Essential Skills
for Papua New Guinea

Spelling

GRADE 4

Peter Durkin

OXFORD

Oxford University Press is a department of the University of Oxford.

It furthers the University's objective of excellence in research, scholarship, and education by publishing worldwide. Oxford is a registered trademark of Oxford University Press in the UK and in certain other countries.

Published in Australia by
Oxford University Press
253 Normanby Road, South Melbourne, Victoria 3205, Australia

First published 2013
Reprinted 2022 (D)

ISBN 978 0 19551842 9

Edited by Emma Short
Cover design by Sarah Hazell
Text design by Sarah Hazell
Typeset by Sarah Hazell
Illustrations by Birdwing Group
Printed and bound in Australia by Ligare Book Printers Pty Ltd

To the Student ›

This book will help you learn about spelling. You will learn:

How to combine letters to make beginnings and endings, for example:

- sh + op = shop
- ca + tch = catch

How to make long vowel sounds, for example:

- rid + e = ride
- r + ai + n = rain

How to spell words with silent letters, for example:

- silent 'k' as in '**knife**'
- silent 'w' as in '**write**'

You will also learn some 'common words'.

They are important because you use them in your writing.
Some common words are difficult to sound out, so you need to practise spelling them every day.

Some examples of common words are:

- have → Do you **have** your lunch with you today?
- because → Kila didn't come to school **because** she was sick.
- far → How **far** do you have to travel to get to town?

Learning to spell can be a challenge but if you work at it, you will get better and better.
After you have finished each unit in this book, think about what you have learnt.
If anything is still a little confusing, ask your teacher for help.
And remember, you will learn to spell unknown or tricky words faster if you practise spelling these words every day.

LOOK, COVER, WRITE, CHECK

Practise your weekly Spelling List this way:

1. **LOOK carefully at the word.**
2. **COVER the word.**
3. **WRITE the word from memory.**
4. **CHECK to see if your spelling is correct.**

CONTENTS ›

Term 1

Term 2

Term 3

	Topic	Focus	Spelling Words	Word Knowledge
21	Vowel digraphs	'ee' words	high, more, never, please, right, jeep, speed, week, sweet, wheel	Syllables
22	Vowel digraphs	'ea' words	seem, name, bit, race, sad, ice cream, clean, please, reach, speak	Syllables
23	Vowel digraphs	'–ow' words (as in 'grow')	book, both, found, live, morning, below, know, show, own, grow	Alphabetical order – 2nd letter
24	Vowel digraphs	'oa' words	night, over, present, shall, day, coat, road, groan, coach, soap	Alphabetical order – 2nd letter
25	Revision	'ee', 'ea', '–ow' and 'oa' words		
26	Vowel digraphs	'ai' words	great, good, air, any, change, brain, sail, paint, paid, afraid	Compound words
27	Vowel digraphs	'–ay' words	my, water, down, first, now, birthday, stay, today, may, play	Compound words
28	Vowel digraphs	'oi' words	think, tree, white, bring, could, spoil, join, noise, boiled, voice	Contractions
29	Vowel digraphs	'oy' words	five, house, mother, soon, too, enjoy, toy, boy, loyal, oyster	Contractions
30	Revision	'ai', '–ay', 'oi' and 'oy' words		

Term 4

	Topic	Focus	Spelling Words	Word Knowledge
31	Vowel digraphs	'aw' words	why, ball, friend, stand, such, thaw, claw, pawpaw, draw, jaw	Adverbs
32	Vowel digraphs	'ew' words	sure, wish, along, brown, carry, flew, knew, new, grew, jewel	Adverbs
33	Vowel digraphs	'ow' words (as in 'cow')	didn't, easy, face, gave, hid, crowd, flower, down, somehow, power	Prepositions
34	Vowel digraphs	'oo' words (as in 'moon')	jump, keep, letter, might, run, cool, tooth, spoon, roof, food	Conjunctions
35	Revision	'aw', 'ew', 'ow' and 'oo' words		
36	Vowel digraphs	'air' words	o'clock, ride, same, second, seven, chair, pair, air, hair, stairs	Antonyms
37	Vowel digraphs	'ar' words	think, walk, yellow, always, buy, smart, mark, party, harm, dark	Synonyms
38	Vowel digraphs	'or' words	clean, door, eight, fall, goes, born, storm, corner, north, force	Prefixes
39	Vowel digraphs	'oo' words (as in 'book')	hear, longer, off, show, third, book, good, stood, wool, shook	Suffixes
40	Revision	'air', 'ar', 'or' and 'oo' words		

To the Teacher >

About the **Essential Spelling Skills** series

The **Essential Spelling Skills** series is a sequential, developmental spelling program that will provide primary students in Grade 3 to 8 with strategies and skills to become independent spellers in English. Each book has been designed as a full year's spelling program consisting of 40 three-page units of work.

Learning to spell strategies

Good spellers use these strategies to help them become successful:

- **Phonological strategies** – how word and letter combinations sound.
- **Visual strategies** – how word and letter combinations look.
- **Morphemic strategies** – how words take different spellings when they change form (for example, church – churches).
- **Etymological strategies** – how words are spelt and where they come from (for example, aeroplane = 'aero' meaning air + 'plane' meaning a flat surface).
- **Inquiry strategies** – how to use learning tools such as a dictionary or thesaurus to spell difficult or unknown words.

These strategies are the basis for learning to spell at every level of this series. In the early levels – Grades 3, 4, and 5 – the emphasis is on visual and phonological strategies to allow children to develop a firm base on which to build more complex understandings of English spelling. In the upper levels – Grades 6, 7 and 8 – there is an increasing emphasis on developing morphemic knowledge and understanding English constructions.

A useful strategy to assist the students' learning, as well as provide the teacher with valuable guidance to students' progress, is the 'Have-A-Go-Card'. To make the simplest 'Have-A-Go-Card', divide a sheet of card or paper into three columns. The students have a go at spelling the word in the first two columns. They tick the spelling they think is correct and check this spelling with their teacher. The teacher confirms the correct spelling and writes it in the third column.

beter ✓	better	better
were	where ✓	where
brake ✓	break	break
realy	really ✓	really
wobling	wobbling ✓	wobbling

How to use the **Essential Spelling Skills** series

This spelling program consists of 40 units of work – ten units per term. Each unit consists of three pages of work including sufficient activities for a five-day spelling program. The first two pages in each unit concentrate on developing spelling strategies to tackle unknown words and the third page allows students to learn more about English, including grammar and writing skills. The units include written activities that are designed to show that spelling is not an isolated skill, but is essential for the development of literacy skills. An assessment program is built into each unit and is usually completed on the fifth day. This is designed to help the teacher test students' spelling knowledge on a regular basis.

Example unit – Term 2 Week 1

The following example shows how a unit of work can be broken down into a week's program using the five spelling strategies. It demonstrates how each unit contains one full week's work relating specifically to spelling, but also incorporates reading and writing.

Unit 11	Focus	Spelling strategy	Teacher preparation	Activities/tasks
Day 1	Long vowel 'a–e' words	Phonological	Make a chart with the Word List or write the Word List on the board. These 'a–e' words need to be displayed for the whole week as this is the unit focus. Write these rules on the board and leave them on display for the whole week: *When vowels are long they say their name.* *The '–e' at the end of the word makes the vowel in the middle say its own name.*	**1.** As a class, read all the words on the Word List and then look at how the '–e' on the end of the word makes the vowel say its own name, for example: hat – hate, mat – mate. **2.** Choose words from the list and ask students to use them (orally) in a complete sentence. **3.** Talk about activities 1 to 4 (orally) before students complete them in the student book. **4.** Students complete the **Off the page** activity to consolidate learning relating to 'a–e' words.
Day 2		Phonological	Copy the '**Sing a Song of Sixpence**' rhyme on a chart or on the board, making it large enough for students to read.	**1.** Reinforce point 1 from Day 1 above. **2.** Talk about activities 4 to 6 (orally) before you ask students to complete them. **3.** Complete the **Rhyme Time** activity to consolidate learning relating to 'a–e' words.
Day 3	There are ten spelling words – five common words and five 'a–e' words.	Visual	Copy the ten spelling words on the board. Students learn these words by applying the strategy: **Look** – at the word **Cover** – the word **Write** – the word **Check** – the spelling	**1.** As a class, read the spelling words. Choose students to use these words (orally) in complete sentences. **2.** Play games with the spelling words to help the students memorise them. For example, ask students to close their eyes and attempt to spell a given word. **3.** Students copy spelling words in their book. **4.** During the week, students need to practice spelling these words. Tell students that these words will be tested at the end of the week.
Day 4		Word knowledge (inquiry strategy)	Copy the definition of a proper noun on the board and leave it for the rest of the week: *Proper nouns are naming words that always begin with a capital letter. They name a person, place or special thing.*	**1.** Reinforce the purpose of a proper noun. **2.** As a class, brainstorm various proper nouns – people, places, animals and special things. **3.** Write the dictated proper nouns on the board. **4.** Students complete the activities in their books.
Day 5	Assessment	Visual and phonological		**1.** Reinforce concepts and skills taught during the week. **2.** Dictate the ten spelling words to students. **3.** Record any relevant assessment information, for example, common errors made by students. **4.** After finishing the spelling test, students complete the Writing activity to extend comprehension and writing skills.

Unit 1

FOCUS > 'sh' words

Word LIST

ship
shop
shift
shelf
shut
shock
sheet
sheep
shirt
shine
shark
shoe
shake
sharp
shell
shout
shoot
fish
dish
wish
wash
cash
dash
mash
sash
crash
flash
smash
ash
brush
crush
hush
mush

1 Copy the **'sh'** table into your book.
Write the words from the Word Bank into the correct box.

Word BANK

brush sheep wipe wish
shape chill shoe flash
cash wash mash jump
shark peach dish sharp
fish shape

'sh' table	
begins with 'sh–'	**ends with '–sh'**
shoe	*fish*

2 Write the words from the Word Bank that are not **'sh'** words in sentences in your book.

3 Choose a word from the Word List for each picture.
Write the words in alphabetical order in your book.

RHYME time > Copy this rhyme into your book and then …

She sells sea shells
On the sea shore
If she sells all the sea shells
On the sea shore
We shall never again see shells
On the sea shore.

1. Underline all the **'sh–'** words.
2. Read the rhyme to a friend as quickly as you can.

4 Choose words from the Word List to fill the gaps.
Write the complete sentences in your book.

a. Jonah caught the _ _ _ _ on his new fishing line.
b. We need a _ _ _ _ _ knife to cut the meat.
c. When the _ _ _ _ hit the rock it sank.
d. You must _ _ _ _ the dishes after dinner.
e. During the storm, I saw the lightning _ _ _ _ _.

5 Write as many words as you can in your book, using the magic word machines.

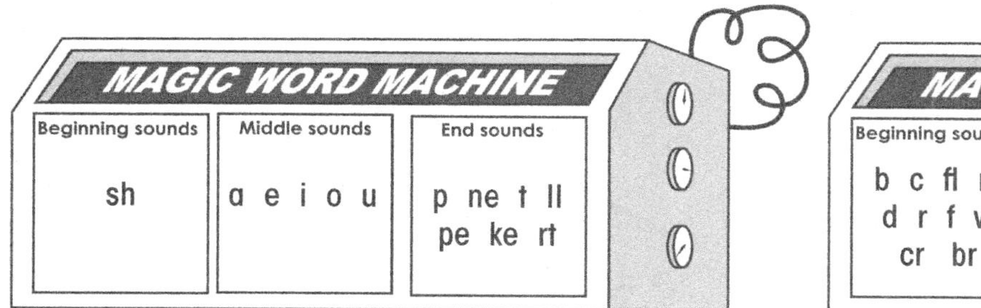

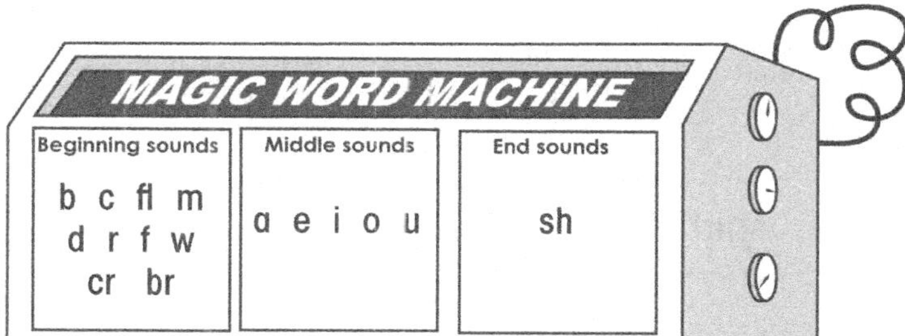

6 Find words from the Word List that have a similar meaning to these words.
Write the words in sentences in your book. The first one has been done for you.

a boat → *ship* *The ship came into port.*

to yell →

a plate →

money →

to hurry →

not open →

7 Write words in your book that rhyme with these words.

a. flash ash ______ ______ ______ ______ ______
b. dish wish ______ ______ ______ ______ ______
c. mush crush ______ ______ ______ ______ ______

8 Choose the correct word. Write the complete sentences in your book.

a. Please (shot / shut) the door.
b. I will (brush / wish) the dog tomorrow.
c. The egg (sheep / shell) broke when it hit the floor.
d. My new (shark / shirt) had a hole in it.
e. The (shoe / shut) was too tight.

WORD KNOWLEDGE › Plurals

✱ RULE

Plural means 'more than one'.
Many plural words end in '**–s**', for example: *two bikes, two cars.*
The words *bikes* and *cars* are both plural.

1 Add '–s' to make the plurals for these words.
Write them in your book.

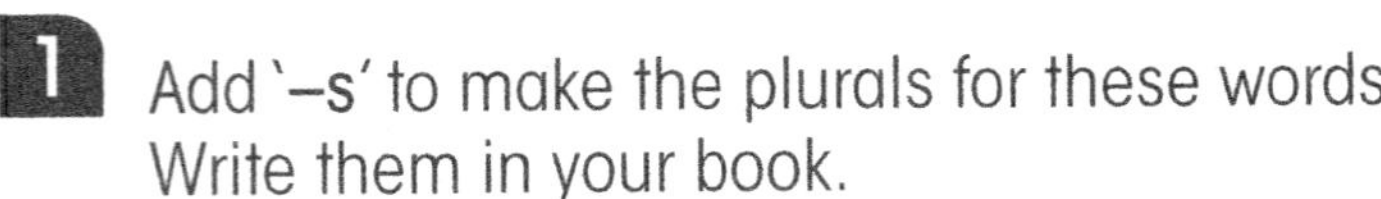

sheet shop shark ship

2 Change these words into plurals.
Write them in sentences in your book.

shirt shell shoe shed shin shovel

COMMON WORDS ›

Choose words from the Spelling List to fill the gaps.
Write the complete sentences in your book.

1. We ___ ___ ___ going to the market today.
2. Can I borrow ___ ___ ___ ___ pencil?
3. The teacher ___ ___ ___ very pleased with your work.
4. I knew that you ___ ___ ___ ___ not feeling well.
5. I would like ___ ___ ___ to come to my party.

Spelling LIST

- are
- was
- you
- were
- your
- shell
- shape
- wish
- smash
- shock

LOOK, COVER, WRITE, CHECK

Practise your weekly spelling this way:

1. LOOK carefully at the word.
2. COVER the word.
3. WRITE the word from memory.
4. CHECK to see if your spelling is correct.

Writing activity

- Imagine you were granted three wishes.
  In three sentences, describe what those wishes would be.

Unit 2

FOCUS › 'ch' words

1 Copy the '**ch**' table into your book.
Write the words from the Word Bank into the correct box.

Word BANK

chill lunch trip chick
slip teach chip bunch
chop torch apple
chunk beach some
child pinch mine

'ch' table	
begins with 'ch–'	**ends with '–ch'**
chip	torch

2 Write the words from the Word Bank that are not '**ch**' words in sentences in your book.

3 Choose a word from the Word List for each picture.
Write the words in alphabetical order in your book.

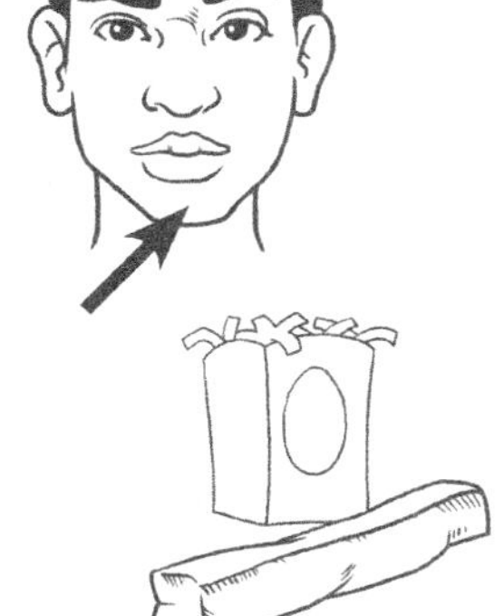

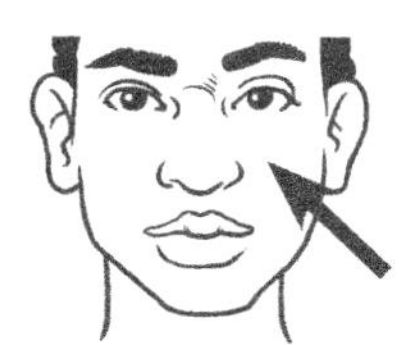

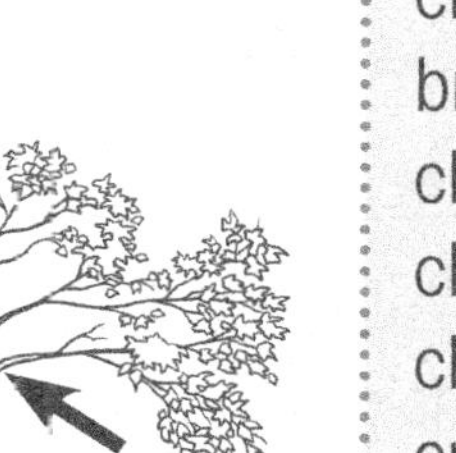

Word LIST

chop
teach
peach
chip
each
chick
beach
cheek
torch
touch
check
pinch
chicken
bunch
child
lunch
chin
bench
chain
branch
chair
church
chill
crunch
punch

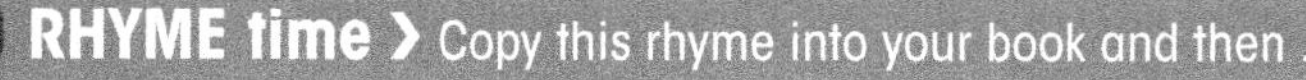

RHYME time › Copy this rhyme into your book and then ...

Underline all the '**–ch**' words.

A pinch and a punch
For the first of the month,
And no returns.
A pinch and a kick
For being so quick.
A slap in the eye
For being so sly.
A pinch and a blow
For being so slow.
Now don't be so fast
Because I'm the last
——— to punch you!

4 Choose words from the Word List to fill the gaps.
Write the complete sentences in your book.

a. We collected shells when we went to the _ _ _ _ _ _.

b. The leg of the _ _ _ _ _ broke when he sat on it.

c. We will _ _ _ _ some wood for the fire.

d. She kissed him on the _ _ _ _ _.

e. A _ _ _ _ _ _ broke from the tree.

5 Write words in your book that rhyme with these words.

a. teach each ________ ________ ________ ________ ________

b. punch crunch ________ ________ ________ ________ ________

6 Write as many words as you can in your book, using the magic word machines.

MAGIC WORD MACHINE

Beginning sounds	Middle sounds	End sounds
ch	a e i o u	p t ke ck w

MAGIC WORD MACHINE

Beginning sounds	Middle sounds	End sounds
b cr l t p	ea en or un in	ch

7 Find words from the Word List that have a similar meaning to these words.
Write the words in sentences in your book. The first one has been done for you.

a twig → *branch* *The children swung on the branch.*

to cut → ____________________

a baby chicken → ____________________

a flashlight → ____________________

a young boy or girl → ____________________

the seaside → ____________________

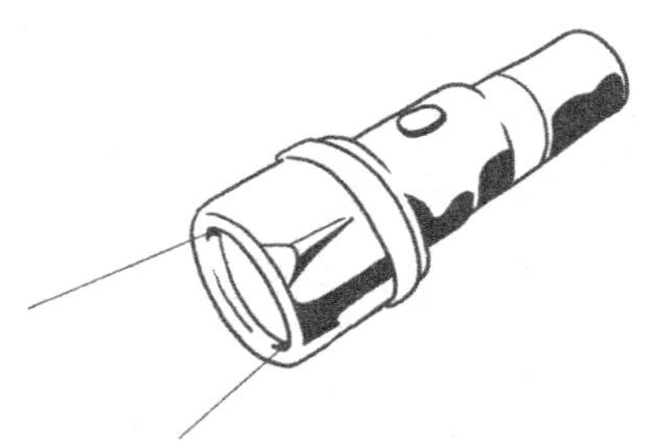

WORD KNOWLEDGE > Plurals

RULE

Most of the time we add '**–s**' to the singular noun to make the **plural**, for example: *huts, schools, lions, creeks.*
We add '**–es**' to nouns that end in '**–ch**', '**–sh**', '**–x**', '**–s**', '**–ss**' or '**–zz**', for example: *boxes, branches, wishes, quizzes.*

1 Add '–s' or '–es' to make the plurals for these words. Write them in your book.

comb dish chicken beach rock match torch chain
cheek church punch brush shirt sash ship peach

2 Change these words into the singular. Write them in sentences in your book.

boxes punches lunches ashes

3 Change these words into plurals. Write them in sentences in your book.

torch branch wish fish

COMMON WORDS >

1 Choose words from the Spelling List to fill the gaps.
Write the complete sentences in your book.

a. John said, "I __ __ __ __ to go home now."
b. The small __ __ __ __ __ began to cry.
c. "Start work now," __ __ __ __ the teacher.
d. There were __ __ __ __ people at the shops today.
e. The __ __ __ __ __ of bananas began to ripen.

2 Write these words in sentences in your book.

chair their other beach

Writing activity

■ Do you think it is ever a good idea to pinch, punch, kick or slap someone? Write your reasons why or why not in your book.

Weekly Spelling List to be tested at the end of the week

Spelling LIST

have
said
many
their
other
child
bunch
chair
chicken
beach

Unit 3

FOCUS > 'th' words

1 Copy the '**th**' table into your book.
Write the words from the Word Bank into the correct box.

Word BANK

teeth shop thick think her
thorn truth mine tenth
path this month they
seven thug both bit

'th' table	
begins with 'th–'	**ends with '–th'**
thick	*teeth*

2 Write the words from the Word Bank that are not '**th**' words in sentences in your book.

3 Choose a word from the Word List for each picture.
Write the words in alphabetical order in your book.

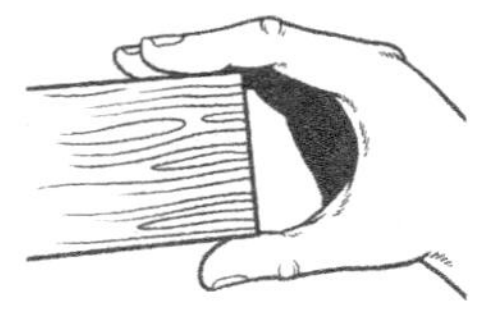
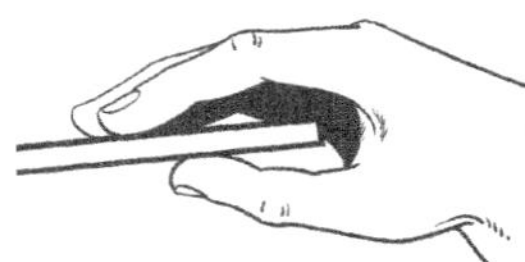
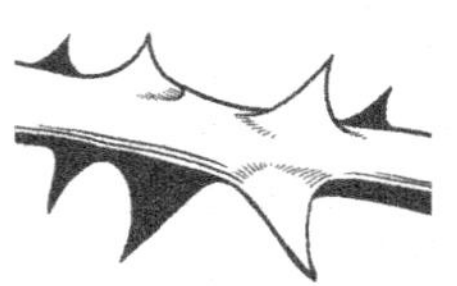
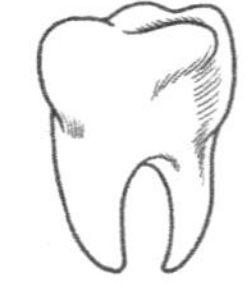

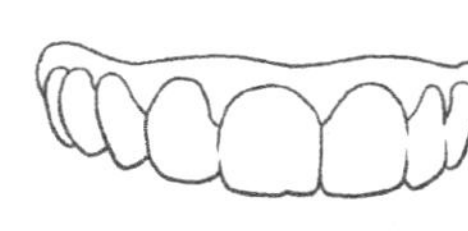

RHYME time > Copy this rhyme into your book and then ...

1. Underline all the '**–th**' words.
2. Riddle: What is the best thing to put in a pie? Your teeth!

When we eat, we use our teeth.
The top teeth meet the teeth underneath!

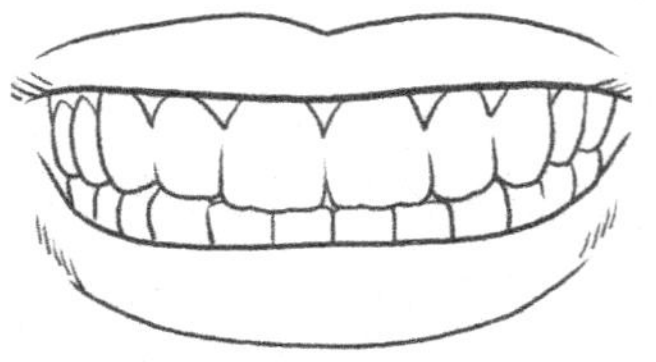

Word LIST

thin
bath
thick
both
thug
teeth
third
tooth
thong
north
thorn
south
think
mouth
then
month
they
truth
the
path
than
fourth
there
them
fifth
they
sixth
that
seventh
this
their
tenth

4 Choose words from the Word List to fill the gaps.
Write the complete sentences in your book.

a. Jill has two buckets, but she cannot find _ _ _ _ _.
b. You must always tell the _ _ _ _ _ _.
c. December is the twelfth _ _ _ _ _ _ of the year.
d. You need a _ _ _ _ _ _ coat when it is cold.
e. The _ _ _ _ _ _ was stuck in his foot.

5 Write these number words in your book.
Use more number words from the Word List to fill the gaps.

first, second, _______, fourth, _______, _______, _______, eighth, ninth, _______

6 Write as many words as you can in your book, using the magic word machines.

MAGIC WORD MACHINE

Beginning sounds	Middle sounds	End sounds
th	a e i	n y t nk rd m

MAGIC WORD MACHINE

Beginning sounds	Middle sounds	End sounds
b s m t p	a o ee oo ou	th

7 Find words from the Word List that have a similar meaning to these words.
Write the words in sentences in your book. The first one has been done for you.

slim, skinny → *thin* *The thin cat slipped through the gap in the fence.*

fat, chunky → ____________

a tub → ____________

the sharp point of a prickly plant → ____________

the part of the face used for eating → ____________

a small walking track → ____________

8 Add '**the–**' to these endings to make '**th–**' words. Write them in your book.

ir
n
se
m
re
y

WORD KNOWLEDGE > Nouns

✱ RULE

A **noun** is a naming word. It is the name of a person, place, animal or thing, for example: *cat, dog, garden, bike.*
Remember, if you can see it, it's a noun.
You can see a cat and a dog. They are nouns.

Look around the classroom. How many nouns, or naming words, can you find? Write at least ten nouns in your book.

COMMON WORDS >

✱ RULE

Tricky spelling – 'their' or 'there'!
Use the word 'their' when you mean 'belonging to them', for example: *their* hats.
Use the word 'there' when you mean 'a place', for example: over *there*.

1 Choose the correct word. Write the words in sentences in your book.

a. We drove (their / there) in our new car.

b. They put (their / there) coats on the hook.

2 Write 'their' and 'there' in sentences in your book.

3 Choose words from the Spelling List to fill the gaps. Write the complete sentences in your book.

a. I won a bronze medal for coming _ _ _ _ _ in the race.

b. Do you think your dad _ _ _ _ _ come to our football match?

c. Jonah wanted to buy _ _ _ _ ice cream from the supermarket.

d. We picked _ _ _ _ pawpaws for dinner.

e. I will _ _ _ _ _ a letter to my cousin tomorrow.

Spelling LIST

there
some
would
write
more
third
their
month
south
bath

Writing activity

- Write a story in your book about washing your pet. Include these nouns: dog water mouth eyes teeth

Unit 4

FOCUS > 'wh–' words

1 Copy the '**wh–**' words from the Word Bank into your book.

Word BANK

teeth whale whip why where win white
week when what woke wing which

2 Write the words from the Word Bank that are not '**wh–**' words in sentences in your book.

3 Choose a word from the Word List for each picture. Write the words in alphabetical order in your book.

Word LIST

wheat
which
whale
whip
why
while
white
which
when
what
wheel
where
whistle
whisker
whisper
whiz
whirlwind
whack
wheelbarrow

RHYME time > Copy this rhyme into your book and then ...

1. Underline all the '**wh–**' words.
2. Circle two more words that begin with '**w–**'.

Way down south where the coconuts grow,
A mouse stepped on an elephant's toe.
The elephant said with tears in his eyes,
'Why don't you pick on someone your own size?'

4 Choose words from the Word List to fill the gaps.
Write the complete sentences in your book.

a. There were _ _ _ _ _ clouds in the sky.
b. Can you tell me _ _ _ you were not at school yesterday?
c. The alarm will go off _ _ _ _ it is time to get up.
d. Do you know _ _ _ _ _ your sister is?
e. The jockey hit the horse with a _ _ _ _.
f. Bread is made from _ _ _ _ _.
g. I don't know _ _ _ _ _ person to pick.
h. The huge _ _ _ _ _ swan flapped its wings.

5 Look at this word puzzle. Find as many '**wh–**' words as you can.
Write them in your book.

a	y	z	w	h	i	s	k	e	v	b	x	c	w	h	y	w	w	h	i	z	e	u	f	v	w	i	l	l	g	s	h	w	h	a	t	r	p

6 Write as many words as you can in your book, using the magic word machine.

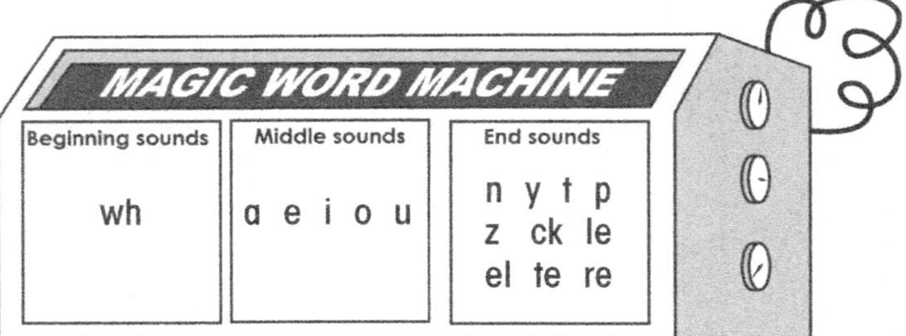

7 Find words from the Word List that have a similar meaning to these words.
Write the words in sentences in your book. The first one has been done for you.

a large sea animal → *whale* *The whale swam out to sea.*

a small cart with one wheel →

used to hit something →

hairs or bristles growing on a face →

the opposite of black →

a plant grown by farmers →

cars, buses and bicycles need these →

WORD KNOWLEDGE > Nouns

RULE

Remember! A **noun** is a naming word.
It is the name of a person, place, animal or thing.

1 Write nouns from the Noun Box in your book to match these pictures.

Noun BOX

fireman
house
lion
pot

2 Look around the playground. Write six nouns in your book for things that you can see.

COMMON WORDS >

1 Choose words from the Spelling List to fill the gaps.
Write the complete sentences in your book.

a. I want a drink of _ _ _ _ _ now.
b. You must stay in your room _ _ _ _ _ _ _ you were naughty.
c. There were a lot of _ _ _ _ _ _ watching the match.
d. I _ _ _ _ _ not jump across the creek.
e. Kila wants everybody to _ _ _ _ to her party.

Spelling LIST

people
could
water
come
because
what
wheel
when
why
whisper

2 Write these words in sentences in your book.

whisper people wheel because

Writing activity

- Write a question beginning with each of these words in your book:
  what when where why

Unit 5

Revision

FOCUS › 'sh' and 'ch' words

Word LIST

ship	chair
fish	beach
chop	chain
teach	sheep
dish	punch
wish	chin
cash	branch
dash	lunch
shop	brush
chip	shirt
mash	ash
flash	shout
peach	bench
each	check
chap	chill
torch	crush
shelf	hunch
shark	hush
chick	brunch
sash	mush

1 Copy this table into your book. Fill the gaps above the double line with words from the Word List. Fill the gaps below the double line with your own words.

Words beginning with 'sh–'	Words ending with '–sh'	Words beginning with 'ch–'	Words ending with '–ch'

2 Write words that rhyme with these words in your book.

fish wish ________ ________ cash ash ________ ________

each peach ________ ________ hunch lunch ________ ________

3 Add to the beginning and ending sounds to make complete words. Use the picture clues to help.

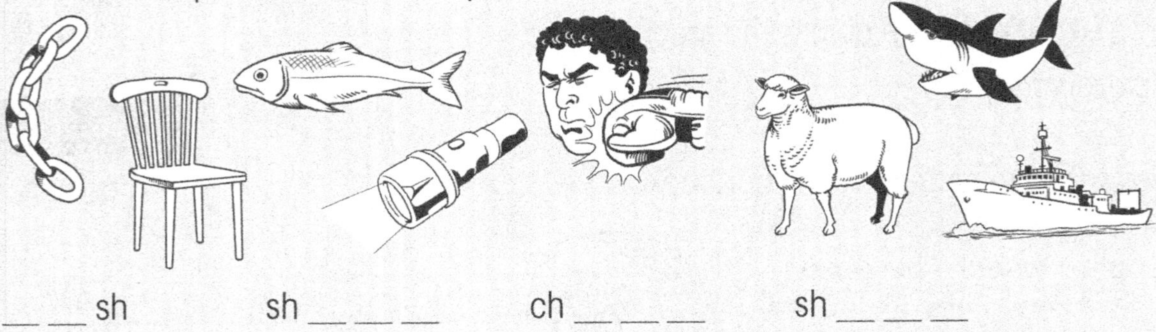

_ _ sh sh _ _ _ ch _ _ _ sh _ _ _

_ _ _ ch ch _ _ _ sh _ _ _ _ _ ch

4 Write each pair of words in a sentence in your book. The first one has been done for you.

shell / beach → *We found a shell on the beach.*

lunch / bench shine / torch shelf / shop

FOCUS > 'th' and 'wh–' words

Word LIST

thin
thick
wheat
why
bath
both
thug
tooth
which
whale
third
thorn
north
south
month
whisker
then
where
third
fifth
whisper
path
sixth
what
wheel
whizz
the
wheelbarrow
whistle
tenth

1 Copy this table into your book. Fill the gaps above the double line with words from the Word List. Fill the gaps below the double line with your own words.

Words beginning with 'th–'	Words ending with '–th'	Words beginning with 'wh–'

2 Add to the beginning and ending sounds to make complete words. Use the picture clues to help.

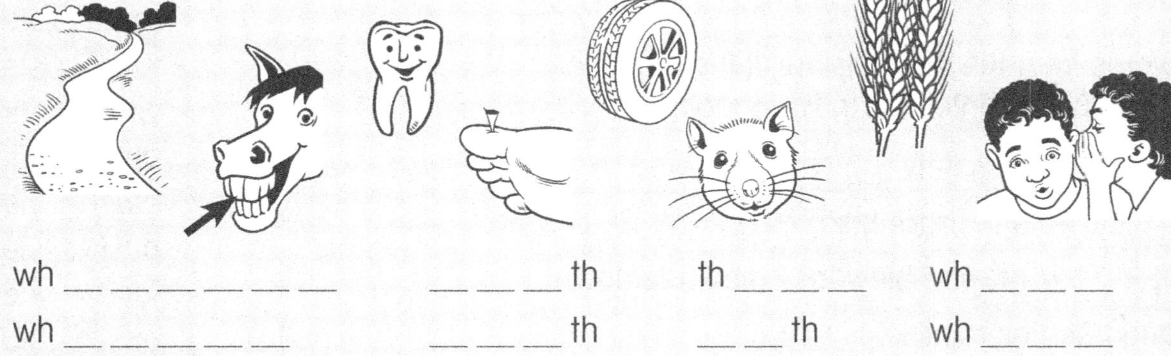

wh __ __ __ __ __ __   __ __ __ th   th __ __ __   wh __ __ __

wh __ __ __ __ __   __ __ __ th   __ __ th   wh __ __ __

3 Fill the gaps with 'th' or 'wh–' words from the Word List.

a. They sat down on __ __ __ carpet.

b. I don't know __ __ __ __ __ I put it.

c. December is the last __ __ __ __ __ of the year.

d. The __ __ __ __ __ of the cart broke.

e. I do not know __ __ __ __ went wrong.

f. She bit the nut and broke her __ __ __ __ __.

4 Write each pair of words in one sentence in your book. The first one has been done for you.

thick / whiskers → *The lion had very thick whiskers.*

mouth / teeth   when / wheel   why / bath   both / whistles   whispering / what

Unit 6

FOCUS > 'st' words

1 Read the '**st**' words in the Word Bank. Copy them into your book.

Word BANK

teeth chest stop twist pram stop star
back stem storm truck frost first

2 Write the words from the Word Bank that are not '**st**' words in sentences in your book.

3 Choose words from the Word List to fill the gaps.
Write the complete sentences in your book.

a. The workman wore a safety __ __ __ __.
b. My friend fell over and broke his __ __ __ __ __.
c. The __ __ __ __ of wind blew the small tree down.
d. The banana tree has a thick __ __ __ __.
e. Students need to __ __ __ __ __ to pass their exams.
f. The sun sets in the __ __ __ __.
g. After the race, we had a __ __ __ __.
h. The __ __ __ __ in the sky twinkled very brightly.
i. We all __ __ __ __ __ when the headmaster comes into our classroom.

Word LIST

chest	rust
nest	trust
pest	cost
rest	lost
test	frost
vest	star
west	start
first	stand
list	state
mist	stem
twist	step
wrist	stick
bust	still
crust	stop
dust	store
just	storm
gust	study
must	

Off the page

■ Use this code breaker to find the missing words. Write the words in your book in complete sentences.

a	b	c	d	e	f	g	h	i	j	k	l	m	n	o	p	q	r	s	t	u	v	w	x	y	z
1	2	3	4	5	6	7	8	9	10	11	12	13	14	15	16	17	18	19	20	21	22	23	24	25	26

(19, 20, 1, 18) (18, 5, 19, 20) (20, 23, 9, 19, 20) (23, 18, 9, 19, 20) (18, 21, 19, 20) (19, 20, 15, 18, 13)

4 Choose the correct word. Write the complete sentences in your book.

a. The bird built its (pest / nest) in spring.
b. I want to eat the bread (crust / dust) first.
c. The (cost / lost) of the book was too much.
d. He put his (twist / fist) through the window.
e. Jonah will do the work in his (dust / study).
f. The sun sets in the (vest / west).

5 Look at this word puzzle. Find as many '**st**' words as you can.
Write them in your book.

m	c	o	s	t	a	j	p	s	t	a	r	z	f	i	s	t	s	r	e	s	t	m	t	s	t	o	p	l	g	s	h	t	e	s	t	r	p

6 Find words from the Word List that have a similar meaning to these words.
Write the words in sentences in your book. The first one has been done for you.

when you can't find the way home → *lost* *I was lost in the forest.*
a part of the body →
a bird's home →
a red traffic sign means ... →
light drizzle →
the hard outer layer on bread →
a school exam →

7 Add '**st–**' to these endings to make '**st–**' words.
Write them in your book in alphabetical order.

and em
ar ep
op udy

8 Add '**–st**' to these beginnings to make '**–st**' words.
Write them in your book in alphabetical order.

twi gu
che pe
tru wri

WORD KNOWLEDGE > Capital letters and full stops

RULE

Capital letters are used for:

- the first letter in a sentence
- names (of people, places days, months, countries, states, towns, rivers)
- the personal pronoun 'I', for example: 'I am going home'.

Full stops are also used to show the end of a sentence.

1 Write this paragraph in your book. Use capital letters and full stops in the correct places.

we had fun at the sing sing mum and dad came with their friends joe and kila we all dressed up in beads and feathers some of the dancers had masks my sister played the kundu drum we went home late it was a lot of fun

COMMON WORDS >

Choose words from the Spelling List to fill the gaps.
Write the complete sentences in your book.

1. We _ _ _ _ _ our teacher if we could go home early.
2. We went to town _ _ _ _ _ school.
3. We heard thunder during the _ _ _ _ _ .
4. "Come over _ _ _ _ ," said the teacher to the naughty boy.
5. "_ _ _ are you going to mend your flat tyre?" asked my mum.

Weekly Spelling List to be tested at the end of the week

Spelling LIST

asked
after
don't
how
here
twist
trust
frost
stand
storm

Writing activity

- Write about a sing sing or a special time in your village. Write about the dancing, the singing, the special clothes and the food. Explain why you think sing sings are good fun.

Unit 7

FOCUS > '–ck' words

1 Read the '**–ck**' words in the Word Bank. Copy them into your book.

Word BANK

teeth pack neck rest sick star sock luck
black still check stick clock stuck

2 Write the words from the Word Bank that are not '**–ck**' words in sentences in your book.

3 Choose words from the Word List to fill the gaps.
Write the complete sentences in your book.

a. The __ __ __ __ __ leading to the village is very narrow.
b. The old car was a complete __ __ __ __ __.
c. The lightning bolt __ __ __ __ __ __ the tree.
d. The building was made of __ __ __ __ __.
e. My sister wore a pretty __ __ __ __ __ to the sing sing.
f. The __ __ __ __ was swimming in the pond.
g. Will you __ __ __ __ __ the cereal boxes on the supermarket shelves?
h. Don't touch electric wires or you will get a nasty __ __ __ __ __.

Word LIST

back	brick
lack	stick
pack	quick
quack	dock
rack	lock
tack	sock
black	tock
crack	block
shack	clock
slack	flock
smack	frock
snack	knock
stack	shock
track	stock
whack	duck
neck	luck
deck	muck
peck	suck
check	tuck
speck	chuck
wreck	pluck
lick	stuck
sick	struck
tick	truck

Off the page

- Copy this sock into your book.
  Colour in all the '**–ck**' words that you can find.

HINT There are more than four words.

a z l i c k
b y o e q r
s t r u c k
d e c k l m i q k
l k k n o c k e o
m w h a c k z b c

4 Find the odd word out in each line. Write it in a sentence in your book.

a.	sick	chick	trick	black	brick
b.	flock	frock	neck	clock	rock
c.	slack	truck	shack	track	crack
d.	sick	stuck	struck	luck	duck
e.	deck	check	wreck	speck	shock

5 Find words from the Word List that have a similar meaning to these words. Write the words in sentences in your book. The first one has been done for you.

good fortune → *luck* *I had a lot of luck to win the lottery.*

the sound a clock makes → ______

a group of birds → ______

a small dot or mark → ______

a large vehicle → ______

to bite with a beak → ______

a small house → ______

6 Use this code breaker to find the missing words. Write the words in your book in complete sentences.

a	b	c	d	e	f	g	h	i	j	k	l	m	n	o	p	q	r	s	t	u	v	w	x	y	z
1	2	3	4	5	6	7	8	9	10	11	12	13	14	15	16	17	18	19	20	21	22	23	24	25	26

a. (19, 14, 1, 3, 11)

b. (3, 8, 21, 3, 11)

c. (3, 18, 1, 3, 11)

d. (2, 12, 15, 3, 11)

e. (17, 21, 9, 3, 11)

f. (18, 1, 3, 11)

RHYME time › Copy this rhyme into your book and then ...

1. Make a list of all of the '**–ck**' words.
2. Circle the words ending in '**–ick**'.
3. Underline the words ending in '**–ack**'.
4. Draw a square around the words ending in '**–ock**'.

Quick! Quick!
The cat's been sick,
And so has the dog,
And Jock, Jack and Nick!
This is bad luck,
That so many are sick.
Poor cat, poor dog,
Poor Jock, Jack and Nick!

WORD KNOWLEDGE > Sentences

RULE

A **sentence** is a group of words that always begins with a capital letter and ends with a full stop, a question mark or an exclamation mark.
Sentences must always make sense.

1 Write these sentences in your book. Use capital letters and full stops in the correct place.

a. her mother came outside
b. the mouse was quick, but the cat was quicker
c. i saw the track in the bush
d. there was a speck of milk on the tablecloth

2 Complete these sentences with your own words. Write them in your book.

a. My name is ___________.
b. I like to eat ___________.
c. It is time to ___________.
d. I want to ___________.

COMMON WORDS >

Choose words from the Spelling List to fill the gaps.
Write the complete sentences in your book.

1. "_ _ _ _ out!" yelled the driver.
2. I went to town with my _ _ _ _ _ _ to buy new shoes.
3. We will visit _ _ _ grandma next week.
4 We told _ _ _ _ not to go swimming because the river was flowing too fast.
5. "Do you want to eat _ _ _ _ sandwich?"

Spelling LIST

look
mother
our
that
them
struck
speck
shock
track
quick

Writing activity

Write answers to these questions in your book.
Make sure each answer is a complete sentence.

1. What is your favourite food?
2. Do you live in a town or a village?
3. How many rooms are there in your house?
4. What games do you play after school?
5. Who does the most work in your family?

Unit 8

FOCUS › '–tch' words

Word LIST

batch
catch
hatch
latch
match
patch
scratch
thatch
fetch
retch
sketch
wretch
ditch
hitch
pitch
witch
switch
botch
notch
blotch
crotch
hutch
clutch
crutch

1 Read the '**–tch**' words in the Word Bank. Copy them into your book.

Word BANK

teeth catch sketch switch smack clutch
crutch clock match truck pitch

2 Write the words from the Word Bank that are not '**–tch**' words in sentences in your book.

3 Choose words from the Word List to fill the gaps.
Write the complete sentences in your book.

a. The sky was _ _ _ _ _ black.
b. We will try to _ _ _ _ _ a ride into town.
c. The _ _ _ _ _ on the chicken coop is very loose.
d. The old man had a red _ _ _ _ _ _ _ on his face.
e. We will build a rabbit _ _ _ _ _ in the school grounds.
f. I hope the egg I bought at the market will _ _ _ _ _ into a chick.

Off the page

- Copy this witch's hat into your book.
  Colour in all the '**–tch**' words that you can find.

HINT There are more than four words.

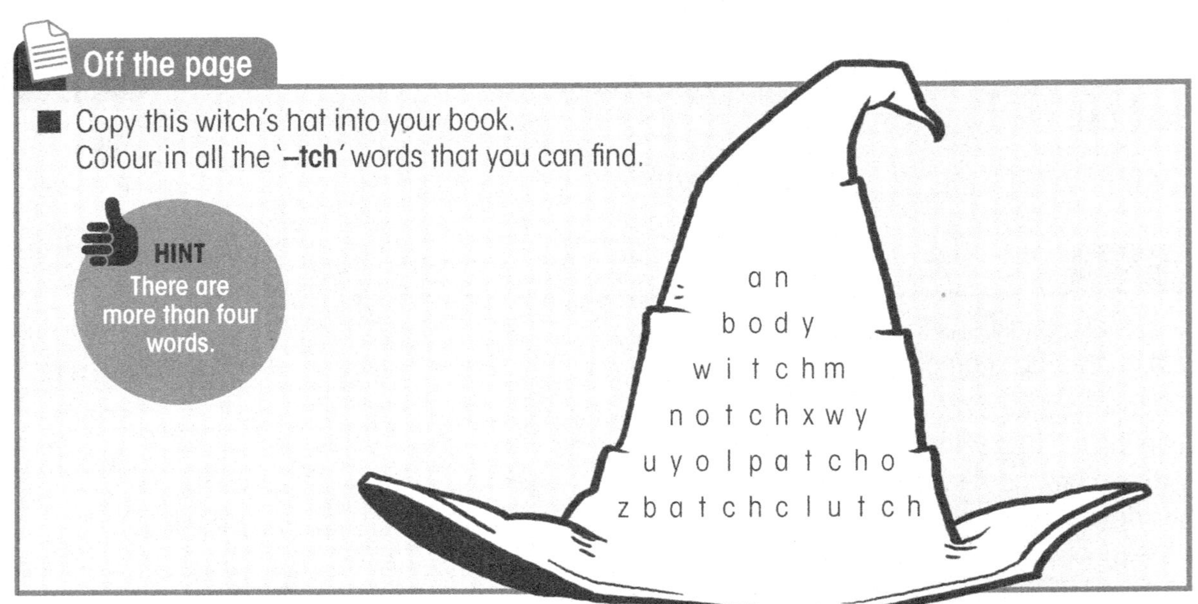

4 Find the odd word out in each line. Write it in a sentence in your book.

a.	batch	catch	match	back	latch
b.	fetch	retch	rich	sketch	wretch
c.	ditch	hitch	pitch	which	witch
d.	botch	notch	hutch	blotch	crotch

5 Find words from the Word List that have a similar meaning to these words. Write the words in sentences in your book. The first one has been done for you.

to turn on electricity → *switch* *I turned on the light switch.*

a house for a rabbit → ____

to break out of an egg → ____

to grab tightly → ____

a roof covering → ____

to bring back → ____

to mend a hole → ____

6 Use this code breaker to find the missing words. Write the words in your book in complete sentences.

a	b	c	d	e	f	g	h	i	j	k	l	m	n	o	p	q	r	s	t	u	v	w	x	y	z
1	2	3	4	5	6	7	8	9	10	11	12	13	14	15	16	17	18	19	20	21	22	23	24	25	26

a. (16, 1, 20, 3, 8)

b. (14, 15, 20, 3, 8)

c. (18, 5, 20, 3, 8)

d. (3, 12, 21, 20, 3, 8)

e. (4, 9, 20, 3, 8)

f. (12, 1, 20, 3, 8)

RHYME time › Copy this rhyme into your book and then ...

1. Complete the missing lines.
2. Underline the words ending in '**–tch**'.

Catch the ball with one hand,
Catch the ball with two.
If it slips through your hands
Out goes you!

Fetch the ball with one hand ...

____
____
____

Clutch the ball with one hand ...

____
____
____

Pitch the ball with one hand ...

____
____
____

WORD KNOWLEDGE › Sentences

RULE

Remember! A **sentence** is a group of words that always has a verb.
Sentences should always make sense.

1 Complete these sentences with verbs from the Verb Box.

a. The angry lion ___________.

b. The green frog _________.

c. The black and white cow ________.

d. The baby kitten _________.

e. The naughty monkey ___________.

f. The wild horse _____________.

Verb BOX

mooed
growled
climbed
purred
jumped
galloped

2 Write complete sentences in your book using these verbs.

swept trotted crawled sang

COMMON WORDS ›

Choose words from the Spelling List to fill the gaps.
Write the complete sentences in your book.

1. _______ are going to town to buy shoes.
2. We like to eat quickly and _______ go out to play.
3. "Is _______ your bag"?
4. We will go fishing _______ it is almost dark.
5. " ________ are you going?" asked our teacher.

Weekly Spelling List to be tested at the end of the week

Spelling LIST

then
they
this
where
when
catch
sketch
witch
notch
hutch

Writing activity

- How do you take care of a pet?
  Write five complete sentences, explaining how you keep a pet happy and healthy.

Unit 9

FOCUS > Double consonant sounds 'bb' 'dd' 'gg' 'rr' 'zz'

1 Copy the double letter table into your book. Write the words from the Word Bank into the correct box.

double letter table				
bb	dd	gg	rr	zz

Word BANK

ladder biggest shine bubble fizz carry juggle rabbit buzz
giggle daddy sorry puzzle kick hurry sorrow dazzle tiger
middle puddle scribble cuddle mum egg

2 Write the words from the Word Bank that do not have double letters in sentences in your book.

3 Choose a word from the Word List for each picture.
Write the words in alphabetical order in your book.

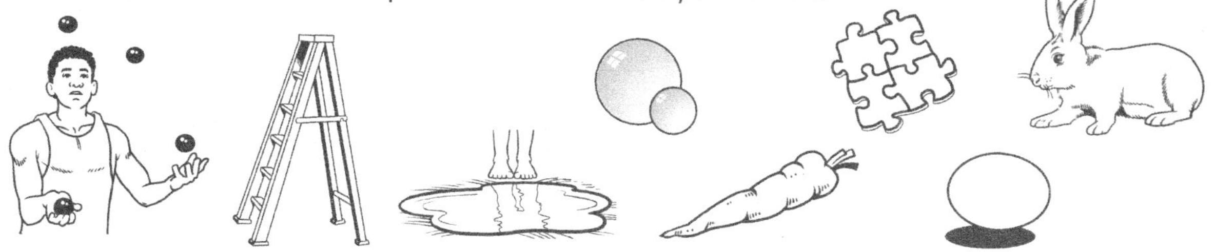

RHYME time > Copy this rhyme into your book and then …

Underline all the '**zz**' words. Can you find the '**dd**' word?

z at the start
like zip zoo zart
zz in the middle
like grizzle, frizzle, drizzle
zz in the end
like buzz, jazz, fizz

Word LIST

bubble
rabbit
cubby
rubber
scribble
rubbish
ladder
cuddle
daddy
puddle
hidden
middle
riddle
giggle
egg
biggest
wriggle
juggle
wagging
carry
carrot
curry
hurry
sorry
carried
sorrow
puzzle
sizzle
buzz
fizzy
muzzle
dazzle

4 Choose words from the Word List to fill the gaps.
Write the complete sentences in your book.

a. We all built a __ __ bb __ house in the tree.
b. The crossword __ __ zz __ __ was hard to solve.
c. Please place the __ __ bb __ __ __ in the bin.
d. We saw the worm __ __ __ gg __ __ across the road.
e. The dog kept on __ __ gg __ __ __ its tail.
f. The teacher said if we don't __ __ rr __ we will miss the bus.
g. The treasure was __ __ dd __ __ under the floor boards.

5 Use double letters to fill the gaps and make words from the Word List.
Write the complete words in your book.

ri__ __le	bu__ __	fi__ __y	gi__ __le	e__ __
da__ __le	la__ __er	da__ __y	wa__ __ing	ca__ __ot
ru__ __ish	hi__ __en	cu__ __y	mi__ __le	so__ __y
bi__ __est	hu__ __y	ca__ __y	si__ __le	pu__ __le

6 Find words from the Word List that have a similar meaning to these words.
Write the words in sentences in your book. The first one has been done for you.

to laugh → *giggle* *The joke made her giggle.*

garbage → ____________

another word for dad → ____________

a jigsaw or crossword → ____________

an orange vegetable → ____________

a hot spicy dish → ____________

7 Write words in your book that rhyme with these words.

a. curry
b. marry
c. jiggle
d. middle
e. sadder
f. grizzle

8 Choose the correct word. Write the complete sentences in your book.

a. I am (hurry / sorry) that I tripped you up.
b. Can you solve the (riddle / middle)?
c. Lean the (carrot / ladder) against the wall.
d. Listen to the sausages (giggle / sizzle) in the pan.
e. The hen laid a big (buzz / egg).

WORD KNOWLEDGE > Statements

RULE

A **statement** is a sentence that gives information about something.
A statement can describe what you feel or think about something.

1 Complete these statements with your own words. Write them in your book.

a. My name is ____________.

b. The month I was born is ____________.

c. My favourite food is ____________.

d. My favourite animal is ____________.

e. The capital city of my country is ____________.

2 Write statements in your book saying what you think or feel about:

a. school holidays
b. telling lies
c. being cruel to animals
d. birthday parties

COMMON WORDS >

Choose words from the Spelling List to fill the gaps.
Write the complete sentences in your book.

1. I climbed _ _ _ _ from the top of the tree.
2. Do you _ _ _ _ who knocked on the door?
3. Lola came _ _ _ _ _ in the race.
4. I would like to find out _ _ _ took the money.
5. You can draw better _ _ _ _ I can.

Spelling LIST

down
first
know
than
who
rubber
middle
biggest
sorry
puzzle

Writing activity

Find an ending for each of these statements.
Write them in your book. Don't forget the full stops!

1. The mouse
2. The shark
3. The wombat
4. The fish
5. The hen
6. The seagulls

...clucked loudly.
...opened its jaws.
...swam away.
...flew over the cliffs.
...dug a burrow.
...ran into its hole.

Revision

FOCUS › 'st', '–ck', '–tch' words

1 Copy this table into your book. Fill the gaps above the double line with words from the Word List. Fill the gaps below the double line with your own words.

Words beginning with 'st–'	Words ending with '–st'	Words ending with '–ck'	Words ending with '–tch'

2 Write words that rhyme with these words in your book.

chest rest ________ ________ black slack ________ ________
dust rust ________ ________ sick tick ________ ________
twist mist ________ ________ batch patch ________ ________

3 Choose 'st', '–ck' or '–tch' words to fill the gaps.
Write the complete sentences in your book.

a. Don't forget to _ _ _ _ the door when you go out.
b. The new TV _ _ _ _ a lot of money.
c. My mother will _ _ _ _ _ the hole in my shorts.
d. You will need a _ _ _ _ _ to light the fire.
e. My teacher is going to _ _ _ _ our spelling today
f. The _ _ _ _ _ of sheep were locked in the paddock.

Word LIST

nest
crutch
rest
lock
lick
star
clock
still
flock
neck
step
test
catch
cost
match
fist
just
fetch
sock
blotch
back
clock
truck
stand
stick
storm
patch

4 Use the picture clues to find words for each picture. Write the words in your book.

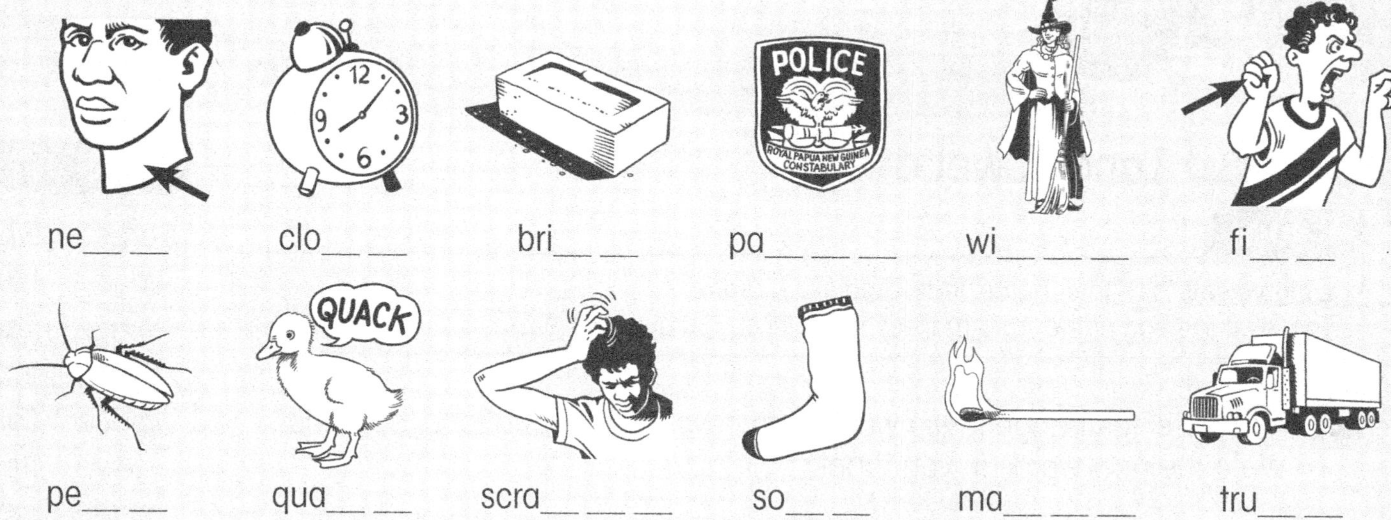

ne__ __ clo__ __ bri__ __ pa__ __ __ wi__ __ __ fi__ __

pe__ __ qua__ __ scra__ __ __ so__ __ ma__ __ __ tru__ __

5 Change one letter in each word to make a new word that matches the clue. Write the new words in your book. The first one has been done for you.

a. snack (hit with hand) *smack*
b. bust (dry powdery dirt)
c. test (time spent sleeping)
d. west (a bed for baby birds)
e. flock (it tells you the time)
f. lick (not feeling well)
g. neck (birds do this to eat food)
h. stack (to glue or paste)
i. cost (not able to find the right way)
j. pitch (a magic woman)
k. luck (makes a quacking noise)

6 Find the odd word out in each circle. Write it in a sentence in your book.

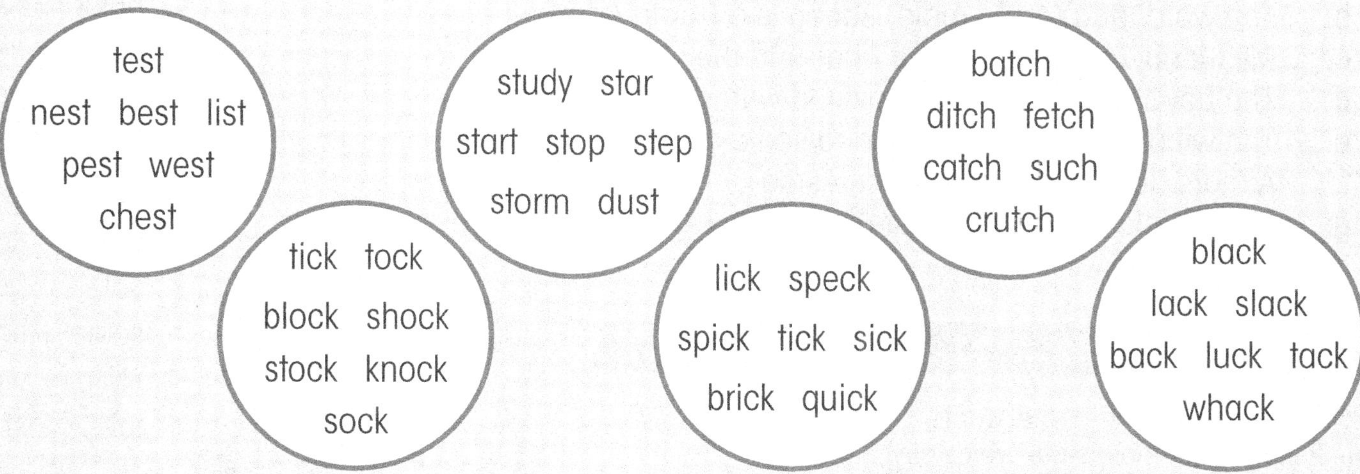

7 Write four of these in your book:

a. five-letter words beginning with '**st–**'
b. five-letter words ending with '**–tch**'
c. five-letter words ending with '**–ock**'
d. five-letter words ending with '**–ack**'
e. four-letter words ending with '**–st**'

Unit 11

FOCUS > Long vowel a–e

RULE

Long vowels 'say' their name, for example: **a** – gr**a**de.
The '**e**' at the end of the word makes the vowel say its own name.

1 Add an '**e**' to change these words into new words with a long 'a' sound. Write the new words in your book.

mad___ can___ cap___ pan___ hat___
pal___ plan___ mat___ sham___

2 Take away the '**e**' to change these words into new words with a short 'a' sound. Are all the new words real words? Write the real words in sentences in your book.

game scrape male bake fade shave rate blame blade

3 Choose the correct word. Write the complete sentences in your book.

a. The farmer broke his (spad / spade) on a hard rock.
b. The word for a (mal / male) sheep is a (rame / ram).
c. My friend wore a large (hat / hate) to the sing sing.
d. The boy's (fac / face) was covered with scratches.
e. The wind was very strong and raised a (gal / gale).
f. A male deer is called a (stage / stag).
g. The athlete's pulse (rat / rate) was very high after the race.

Word LIST

ace	whale
face	blame
grace	came
pace	fame
place	flame
race	frame
blade	game
fade	cane
grade	crane
made	lane
shade	pane
spade	plane
cage	ape
page	cape
rage	grape
stage	scrape
wage	shape
bake	crate
brake	date
cake	gate
fake	hate
lake	late
gale	cave
sale	gave
scale	save
stale	wave
tale	shave

RHYME time > Copy this rhyme into your book and then ...

1. Underline all the '**–ate**' words.
2. Write four more '**–ate**' words of your own.

Sing a song of sixpence
Piled on a plate,
Three happy children
Swinging on a gate.

When the gate was opened
They all sat down and ate.
What a silly thing to do
On the garden gate.

4 Copy this table into your book. Write rhyming words of your own in the correct row.

face	place	race			
skate	mate	plate			
make	shake	wake			
sale	tale	whale			
blame	same	game			

5 Find words from the Word List that have a similar meaning to these words. Write the words in sentences in your book. The first one has been done for you.

like a monkey → *ape* *The ape loves to eat bananas.*

the front of your head →

a tool for digging →

a very strong wind →

a large sea animal →

this flies people through the air →

a man is a ... →

the opening in a fence →

not real →

6 Write as many words as you can in your book, using the magic word machine.

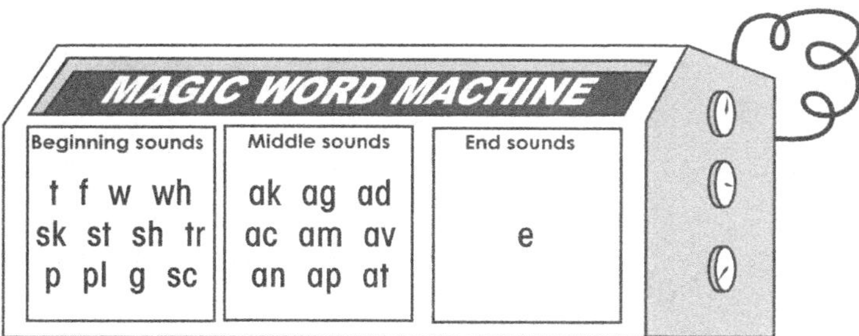

7 Find the words in these puzzles. Write them in your book.

a. s
c a

b. f
l a

c.
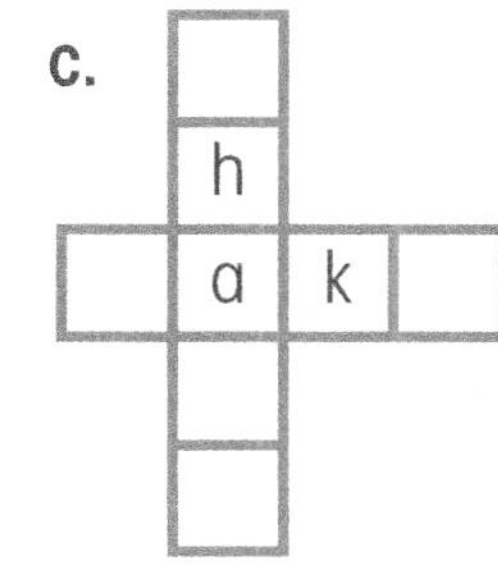

d. a
m

WORD KNOWLEDGE › Proper nouns

✻ RULE

Proper nouns are special nouns that always begin with a capital letter.
They name a person, place or special thing.
For example: *Lea* (person), *Lae* (place), *Parliament House* (special thing).

1 Copy this story into your book. Use capital letters for the proper nouns.

Last week mum, my sister sal and I went to the market in port moresby. We bought a bilum for my sister and a table for grandpa joe.

In the afternoon we had lunch with our friend lia. She bought some food for her pet dog tibbles and her pet cat dribbles.

It was late before we went home and we were very tired when at last we arrived at our village. It was a good day. We all enjoyed our time at port moresby.

COMMON WORDS ›

1 Choose words from the Spelling List to fill the gaps.
Write the complete sentences in your book.

a. We had to go __ __ __ __ to get the keys.
b. The teacher had to __ __ __ __ out very loudly.
c. Mum gave __ __ __ __ of us an ice cream.

2 Write these words in sentences in your book. also dear

3 Draw a picture for each of these groups of words in your book.
Write the words under each picture.

a. cage bird fly
b. brake car crash
c. plane taxi land

Writing activity

- Write a story in your book about when you went to the market.
Write about who you went with, where it was and what you bought.
Don't forget the capital letters for all the proper nouns in your story.

Spelling LIST

also
back
call
dear
each
face
cage
brake
plane
made

Unit 12

FOCUS > Long vowel i–e

RULE

Long vowels 'say' their name, for example: **i** – bride.
The '**e**' at the end of the word makes the vowel say its own name.

1 Add an '**e**' to change these words into new words with a long 'i' sound. Write the new words in your book.

pin___ sit___ kit___ dim___ spic___
hid___ crim___ grim___ slim___

2 Take away the '**e**' to change these words into new words with a short 'i' sound. Are all the new words real words?
Write the real words in sentences in your book.

stripe quite bite wine side ride wife pike bike

3 Choose the correct word. Write the complete sentences in your book.

- **a.** My grandpa is a very (was / wise) old man.
- **b.** My painting won first (prize / prise) at the craft market.
- **c.** The river was very (wade / wide) and too dangerous to cross.
- **d.** The girl wore a (which / white) dress to school.
- **e.** The bananas on the tree were (rope / ripe) and ready to be picked.
- **f.** The old man had a crooked (spin / spine).

RHYME time > Copy this rhyme into your book and then ...

1. Underline all the '**–ile**' words.
2. Write four more '**–ile**' words of your own.

She smiled at a monkey,
She smiled at a fly,
She smiled at an elephant
Galloping by.
And then she smiled
at a CROCODILE!

So ...
You can smile at monkeys,
You can smile at flies,
You can smile at elephants
Galloping by.
BUT NEVER smile at a crocodile.

Word LIST

dice	smile
ice	stile
lice	rise
mice	wise
nice	prize
price	size
rice	life
spice	wife
bride	crime
glide	dime
guide	grime
hide	slime
pride	dine
ride	nine
side	pine
slide	spine
wide	swine
bike	twine
hike	wine
like	bite
pike	quite
spike	site
strike	sprite
file	white
mile	gripe
pile	ripe
	pipe

4 Copy this table into your book. Write rhyming words of your own in the correct row.

dine	fine	mine			
kite	spite	write			
gripe	ripe	stripe			
mice	twice	spice			
hide	glide	ride			
like	bike	strike			

5 Find words from the Word List that have a similar meaning to these words. Write the words in sentences in your book. The first one has been done for you.

a long walk → *hike* *We like to hike in the mountains near our village.*

a kind of strong string → ____

a kind of small fairy → ____

used to flavour food → ____

a girl getting married → ____

a woman with a husband → ____

an alcoholic drink → ____

the number after eight → ____

6 Write as many words as you can in your book, using the magic word machine.

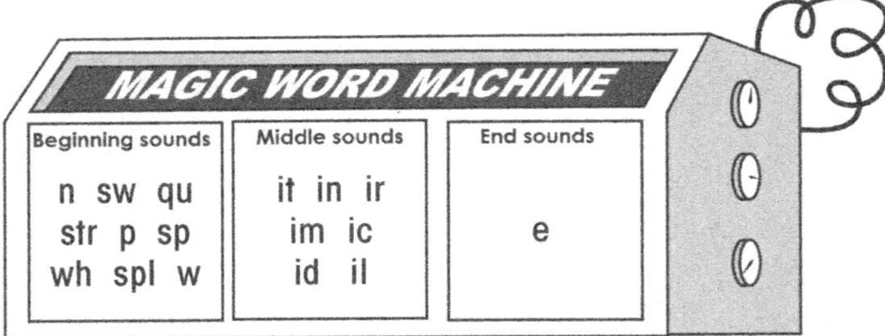

7 Find the words in these puzzles. Write them in your book.

a. p, e

b. d, i

c. p, i, k

d. s, i

WORD KNOWLEDGE > Proper nouns

RULE

Remember! **Proper nouns** are special nouns that always begin with a capital letter. They name a person, place or special thing.

1 Write these sentences into your book. Use capital letters for the proper nouns.

a. Tai lives in bougainville.
b. My sister went to lae.
c. Port moresby is the capital of papua new guinea.
d. The river fly flows past our village.
e. A high mountain in papua new guinea is albert edward.

2 Copy and complete this chart in your book.
Remember that names are proper nouns and need a capital letter.

Your first name	
A friend's name	
Your birthday month name	
Your parents' names	
Your teacher's name	
Your pet's name	
Your village's name	

COMMON WORDS >

Choose words from the Spelling List to fill the gaps.
Write the complete sentences in your book.

1. What __ __ __ __ of ice cream do you like to eat?
2. The name of the __ __ __ __ was Josie.
3. The ball hit the small boy on his __ __ __.
4. The man travelled to his __ __ __ __ by canoe.
5. "How __ __ __ can you jump?" asked our teacher.

Spelling LIST

ear
far
girl
home
kind
vine
spice
strike
write
fire

Writing activity

- What do you think is the most frightening animal in Papua New Guinea? Is it a crocodile? Draw and write a description of it in your book. Explain why you think it is scary.

Unit 13

FOCUS > Long vowel o–e

RULE

Long vowels 'say' their name, for example: **o** – h**o**pe.
The '**e**' at the end of the word makes the vowel say its own name.

1 Add an '**e**' to change these words into new words with a long 'o' sound. Write the new words in your book.

mop___ hop___ ton___ lop___ pop___
slop___ scop___ zon___ cop___

2 Take away the '**e**' to change these words into new words with a short 'o' sound. Are all the new words real words?
Write the real words in sentences in your book.

tone hope gnome rope stone slope pope bone hose

3 Choose the correct word. Write the complete sentences in your book.

a. The plate (broke / joke) when she dropped it.
b. The clown had a very large (bone / nose) on his face.
c. The man fell down the steep (slop / slope).
d. The truck driver used a thick (rope / ripe) to tie his load.
e. He watered his garden using a long (rose / hose).
f. I made a clay (gnome / chrome) at school and put it in our garden at (home / dome).
g. He (awoke / spoke) when he smelt (stone / smoke) in the house.

Word LIST

bloke	froze
broke	bone
choke	clone
joke	cone
poke	drone
smoke	lone
spoke	phone
stroke	prone
woke	stone
awoke	throne
chrome	tone
dome	zone
gnome	cope
home	grope
nose	hope
hose	lope
pose	mope
prose	pope
rose	rope
those	scope
chose	slope
doze	elope

RHYME time > Copy this rhyme into your book and then …

1. Underline all the '**–ose**' words.
2. Find an '**–ise**' word and write it in your book.

The wise man chose
To plant a rose.
The bad boy chose
To pick his nose.

Which one of those
Is better?
The nose I suppose!

4 Copy this table into your book. Write rhyming words of your own in the correct rows.

joke	poke	spoke			
rose	those	chose			
phone	zone	tone			
cope	lope	scope			
chrome	gnome	dome			

5 Find words from the Word List that have a similar meaning to these words. Write the words in sentences in your book. The first one has been done for you.

a shape → *cone* *I like to eat ice cream in a cone.*

a funny story →

the place where you live →

a small rock →

someone said something →

smashed to pieces →

something was as cold as ice →

a king sits on this →

a fragrant flower →

6 Write as many words as you can in your book, using the magic word machine.

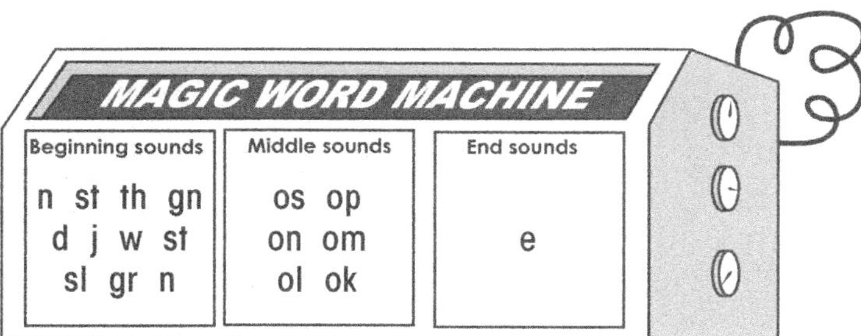

7 Find the words in these puzzles. Write them in your book.

a.

		s		
s		o		

b.

		c		
		o		

c.

	p		
	o		
	k		

d.

		n		
s		o		

WORD KNOWLEDGE > Adjectives

RULE

An **adjective** is a describing word that tells more about a noun, for example: a *pink* rose, a *large* balloon.

Adjective BOX

noisy
fat
woolly
spotty
busy
stripy

1 Choose the best adjective from the Adjective Box to describe each animal. Write the adjectives and nouns in your book.

dog sheep zebra beetle bee pig

2 Use these adjectives to write sentences of your own in your book.

huge tiny hot cold happy sad kind cruel

COMMON WORDS >

1 Choose words from the Spelling List to fill the gaps. Write the complete sentences in your book.

a. There were many __ __ __ __ __ __ at the sing sing.
b. I have __ __ __ __ one sister.
c. I came __ __ __ __ in the sprint race.
d. "What is your __ __ __ __ ?" asked our teacher.
e. The outdoor table was __ __ __ __ of wood.

Spelling LIST

last
made
name
only
people
smoke
phone
rope
choke
home

2 Write these words in sentences in your book.

home rope phone

3 Write the words from the Spelling List in alphabetical order in your book.

Writing activity

- Choose an animal such as a dog, a pig or a wild animal that lives in the bush near you. Write a description of your animal – what it looks like, where it lives, what it likes to eat. Make sure you use plenty of adjectives to describe it.

FOCUS > Long vowel u–e

RULE

Long vowels 'say' their name, for example: **u** – r**u**d**e**.
The '**e**' at the end of the word makes the vowel say its own name.

1 Add an '**e**' to change these words into new words with a long 'u' sound. Write the new words in your book.

fus___ cut___ rud___ flut___ lut___
amus___ exclud___ rul___ Jun___

2 Take away the '**e**' to change these words into new words with a short 'u' sound. Are all the new words real words?
Write the real words in sentences in your book.

cute rude use fuse June rule

3 Choose the correct word. Write the complete sentences in your book.

a. We must not (pollute / salute) our environment.
b. The clown had a very (cute / chute) face.
c. My favourite (juice / juic) is pineapple.
d. We must (use / fuse) fresh water for drinking.
e. The boy was very (crude / rude) to his teacher.
f. We (us / use) water to mix our paints.
g. We (pollute / salute) the flag when we sing the national anthem.

RHYME time > Copy this rhyme into your book and then ...

Underline all the '**–ude**' words.

Little Jack Horner sat in the corner
Eating his Christmas pie.
He thought it was rude
To sit in the nude
So he put on his old school tie.

Word LIST

rude
nude
crude
exclude
include
intrude
brute
chute
cute
flute
lute
mute
pollute
salute
parachute
use
fuse
muse
ruse
accuse
amuse
confuse
abuse
excuse
misuse
June
dune
prune
rule

4 Copy this table into your book. Write rhyming words of your own in the correct row.

crude	exclude	include		
lute	chute	brute		
amuse	confuse	ruse		
dune	prune	June		

5 Find words from the Word List that have a similar meaning to these words. Write the words in sentences in your book. The first one has been done for you.

something you must obey → *rule*

There is a school rule that says you cannot hit others.

wearing no clothes →

to forgive someone →

the sixth month of year →

a dried plum →

mixed up in the mind →

not polite →

a musical instrument →

a sand hill →

6 Write as many words as you can in your book, using the magic word machine.

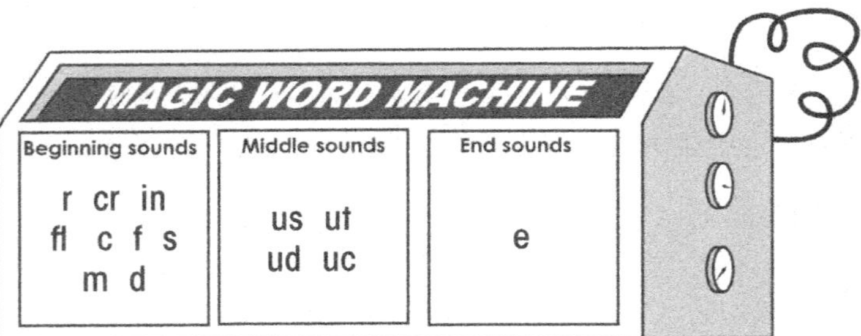

7 Find the words in these puzzles. Write them in your book.

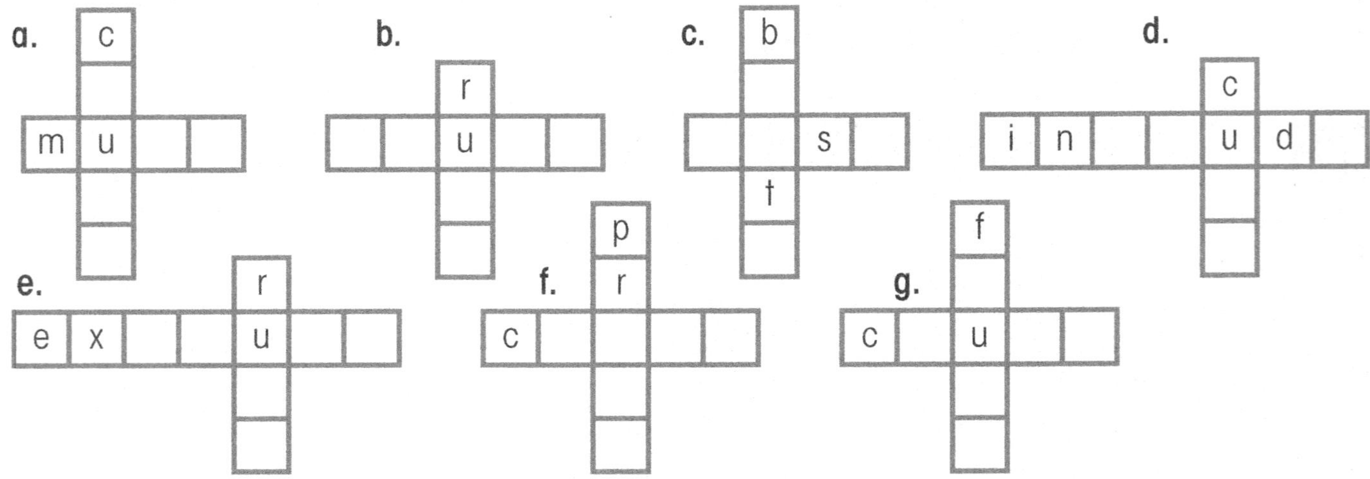

WORD KNOWLEDGE > Adjectives and nouns

RULE

Remember! A **noun** is a naming word and an **adjective** is a describing word.
The adjective tells us more about the noun.

Choose the best adjective from the Adjective Box to describe each noun.
Write the adjectives and nouns in your book.

car man house cat rose jumper dog cup

ADJECTIVE BOX

large
old
beautiful
happy
furry
broken
shaggy

COMMON WORDS >

1 Choose words from the Spelling List to fill the gaps.
Write the complete sentences in your book.

a. The boys __ __ __ __ to go to the oval to play soccer.
b. There were many coconuts __ __ __ __ __ the tree.
c. He __ __ __ home quickly because it was going to rain.
d. The elders __ __ __ that we need to work hard at school.
e. "__ __ __ __ me why you are late," said our teacher.

2 Write these words in sentences in your book.

flute rule fuse

3 Write the words from the Spelling List in alphabetical order in your book.

Weekly Spelling List to be tested at the end of the week

Spelling LIST

ran
say
tell
under
want
crude
fuse
rule
intrude
flute

Writing activity

■ Read this description of a sister.
Write all the nouns in blue and all the adjectives in red in your book.

My big sister has short, curly hair. She has big brown eyes and a smiling mouth.
Her favourite shirt is pale blue. She loves wearing her old denim jeans.
After dinner, she sits down by the fire and drinks a nice, cold cup of pineapple juice.
She has a very loud laugh and loves telling jokes to her friends.

Revision

FOCUS › Long vowel a–e, i–e, o–e, u–e words

1 Add an '–e' to change these words into new words with a long vowel sound. Write the new words in your book.

hat → ______	mat → ______	pin → ______	kit → ______
mop → ______	pop → ______	slid → ______	rag → ______
cut → ______	grim → ______	cop → ______	mad → ______

HINT
Remember!
The '–e' at the end of a word makes the vowel say its own name.

2 Take away the '–e' to change these words into new words with a short vowel sound. Are all the new words real words? Write the real words in your book.

pine slide slope lice bake lone prune mope
ride mile hate cute June hope use fame

HINT
Be careful!
Not all the words are real when you take away the '–e'.

3 Choose the correct word. Write the complete sentences in your book.

a. The wind blew the (kit / kite) high in the sky.
b. The cat sat on the (mate / mat) while the dog ate his (bon / bone).
c. The (pine / pin) tree dropped cones on the ground.
d. The wheel rolled down the (slop / slope).
e. He (cute / cut) the coconuts down with a knife.
f. Dorcas (mad / made) the cake in the oven.
g. She wanted to (hid / hide) behind the tree.

4 Write as many words as you can in your book, using the magic word machine.

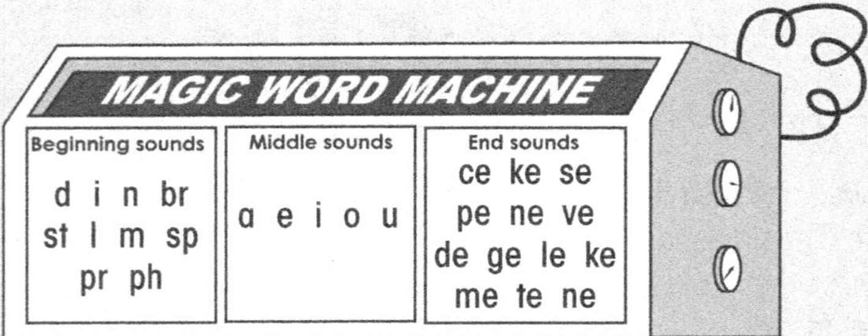

5 Find the words in these puzzles. Write them in your book.

a.

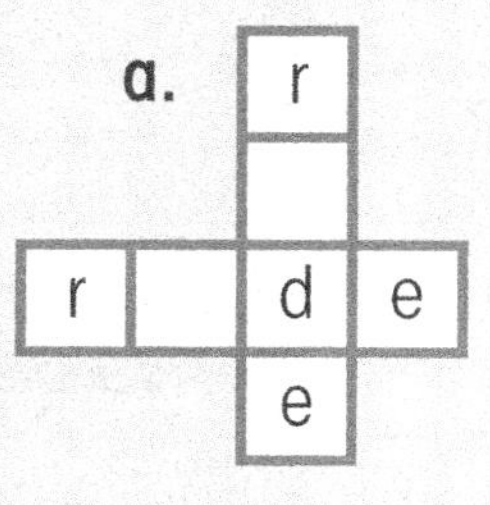

b.

c.

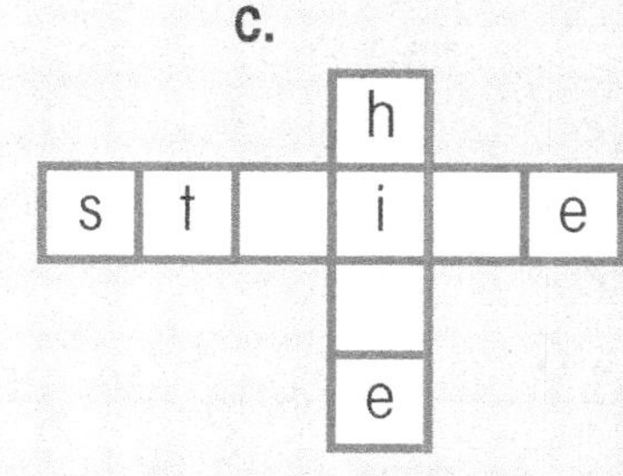

d.

6 Copy this table into your book. Write rhyming words of your own in the correct row.

pine	nine	fine		
blade	fade	made		
mute	chute	salute		
quite	site	sprite		
chose	those	hose		
ace	race	place		

7 Find words from the Word Bank that have a similar meaning to these words. Write the words in sentences in your book. The first one has been done for you.

it flies in the sky → *plane* *The plane landed at Lae.*

to really dislike →

a dog chews on this →

it has two wheels →

you smell with it →

small rodents →

a funny story →

an act against the law →

wearing no clothes →

Word BANK

mice nose joke nude hate bone crime bike plane

8 Find the odd word out in each line. Write it in a sentence in your book.

a.	fine	line	pine	pane	mine	spine
b.	brute	cute	lute	flute	fuse	mute
c.	spice	nice	rice	ice	prize	dice
d.	bride	glide	ride	side	rid	wide
e.	blade	fade	made	shade	mad	spade

Unit 16

FOCUS > Long 'i' ('y') sound

1 Choose the correct word. Write the complete sentences in your book.

a. We will (dry / fry) the fish in a pan over the open fire.
b. My brother will (dry / try) very hard to learn his spelling words.
c. My sister asked me (try / why) I won't play with her.
d. (By / My) teacher told my mum that I was naughty in class.
e. My dad told me to (why / try) very hard at school.

2 Find the words for these pictures in the Word List.
Write them in your book.

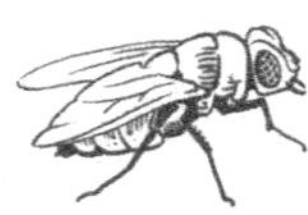

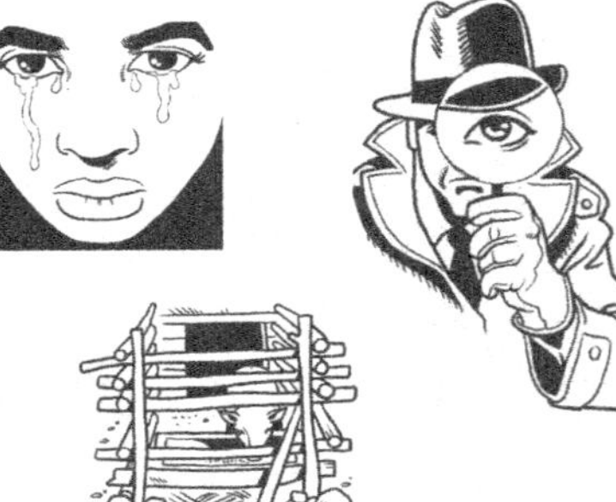

3 Choose words from the Word List to fill the gaps.
Write the complete sentences in your book.

a. The storm clouds made the __ __ __ look very dark.
b. My birthday is in the month of __ __ __ __.
c. The baby will __ __ __ if you don't give her some food.
d. The pig's house is called a __ __ __.

Word LIST

by
cry
dry
fly
fry
my
pry
shy
sky
sly
spy
sty
try
why
deny
July
guy
butterfly
pigsty
blowfly
myself
smile

RHYME time > Copy this rhyme into your book and then ...

1. Underline the words ending in '**–y**'.
2. Circle a word ending in '**–e**' that rhymes with 'cry'.

Cry baby, cry
Poke him in the eye
Hang him on the lamp post
Leave him there to dry.

4 Copy this table into your book. Change one letter in each word to make a new word. Write the new words in sentences in your book.

dry	shy	sly	cry

5 Find the words in these puzzles. Write them in your book.

a.

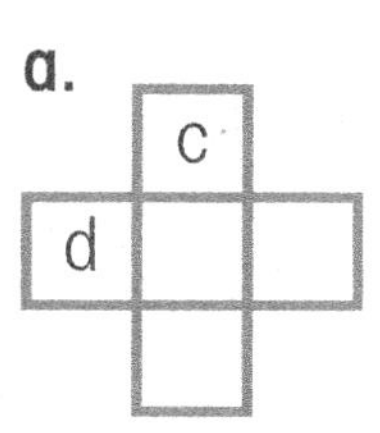

b.

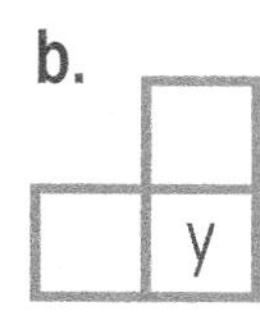

c.

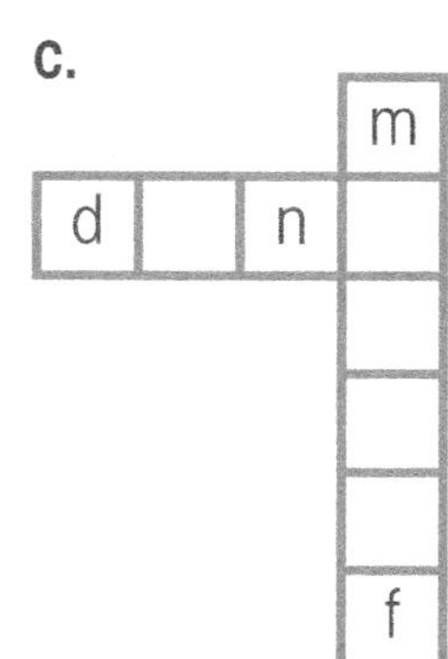

d.

w

p s

6 Find words from the Word List that have a similar meaning to these words. Write the words in sentences in your book. The first one has been done for you.

a pig pen → *sty* *The farmer put the pigs in the sty.*

the seventh month of the year → ______

to weep or shed tears → ______

a word that starts a question → ______

not wet → ______

a pesky insect → ______

a flying insect → ______

to make an effort → ______

timid → ______

7 Use the beginning sounds to write '–y' words. The first one has been done for you.

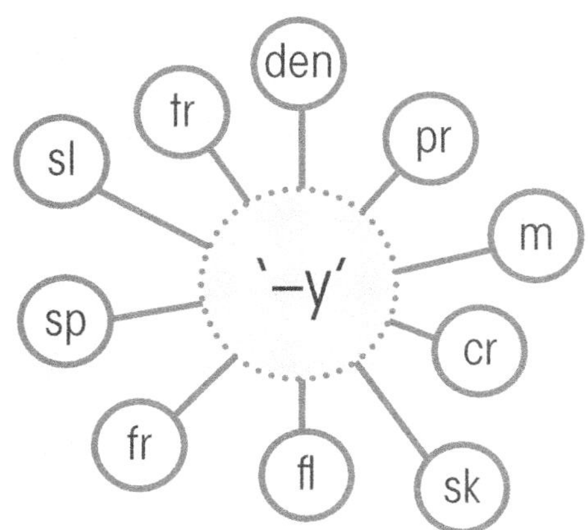

sly ______ ______

WORD KNOWLEDGE > Nouns and pronouns

RULE

Remember! A **noun** is a naming word, for example: *boy, girl, tiger.*
A **pronoun** is used in place of a noun, for example: *he, she, it.*
The girl is brave – 'girl' is a noun.
She is brave – 'she' is a pronoun.

PRONOUN BOX

I
he
it
they
him
you
she
we
me
her

1 Choose pronouns from the Pronoun Box to fill the gaps.
Write the complete sentences in your book.

a. The mother tiger fed _ _ _ cub and then she went to sleep.
b. The mother tiger is clever and _ _ _ is also brave.
c. The father tiger eats when _ _ is hungry.
d. We can see tigers when _ _ go to the zoo.
e. If tigers don't catch their prey, _ _ _ _ won't survive.

2 Rewrite these sentences in your book.
Use a pronoun from the Pronoun Box to replace the underlined words.

a. Tiny is a pet and Tiny likes to bark.
b. The teacher was angry and the teacher yelled at us.
c. Mother and Father were hungry, but Mother and Father didn't eat anything.
d. The cat sat on a pin and the cat ran up the curtains.

COMMON WORDS >

Weekly Spelling List to be tested at the end of the week

Choose words from the Spelling List to fill the gaps.
Write the complete sentence in your book.

1. Next _ _ _ _ I will be in Grade 8.
2. She wore her _ _ _ _ dress to the sing sing.
3. My grandpa _ _ _ _ from his village to visit us.
4. I need to _ _ _ _ my school bag before I can go home.
5. We will go to town _ _ _ _ _ _ _ day.

Spelling LIST

year
another
best
came
find
guy
why
July
deny
fry

Writing activity

- If you had a choice of how old you would like to be, write why you would like to be that age and describe how your life would be different.

FOCUS › '–ight' words

1 Choose the correct word. Write the complete sentences in your book.

a. The loud thunder gave him a (flight / fright).
b. The (night / knight) wore silver armour.
c. The girl wore very (right / tight) jeans to the party.
d. Our teacher told us that we must not (fright / fight) at school.
e. The morning (bright / light) was very (plight / bright).
f. The (slight / sight) of food made the poor man very hungry.

Word LIST

bright
fight
flight
fright
knight
light
might
night
plight
right
sight
slight
tight
brighter
frighten

2 Find the words for these pictures in the Word List. Write them in your book.

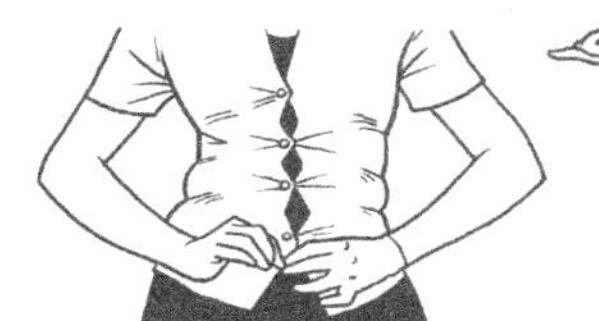

3 Find the words in these puzzles. Write them in your book.

a.

f
m i

b.

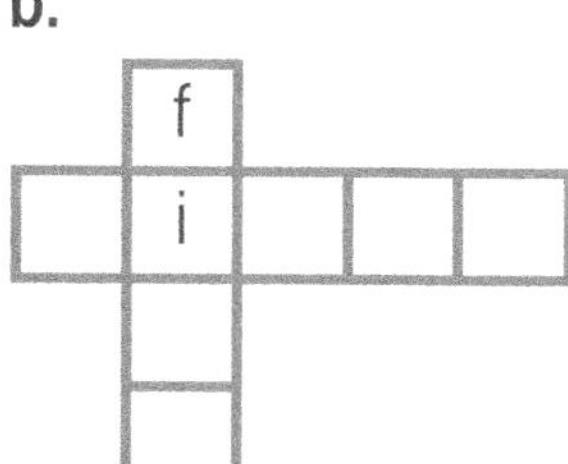

c.

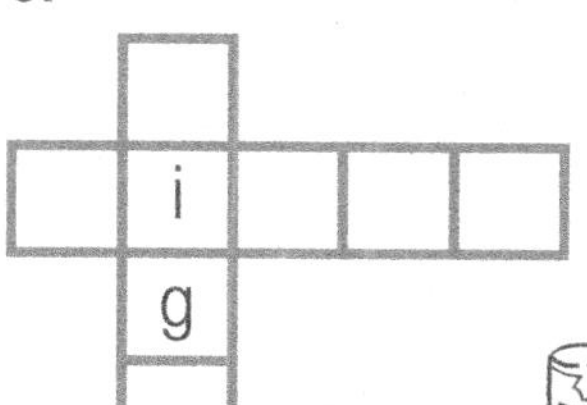

d.

n
i

RHYME time › Copy this rhyme into your book and then ...

1. Underline the '**–ight**' words.
2. Circle an '**–ite**' word that rhymes with 'night'.
3. Write four more '**–ight**' or '**–ite**' words of your own.

Night night, sleep tight,
Don't let the bed bugs bite.

If they bite,
Squeeze them tight,

And they won't bite
Another night.

4 Choose words from the Word List to fill the gaps.
Write the complete sentences in your book.

a. The morning _ _ _ _ _ _ shone through my window.

b. The _ _ _ _ _ _ of the old woman crying made me feel sad.

c. I was sitting on the seat but he walked _ _ _ _ _ _ past me.

d. My friend has a sore head because he was involved in a _ _ _ _ _ _.

5 Copy this table into your book. Change one letter in each word to make a new word.
Write the new words in sentences in your book.

light	night	sight	fight

6 Find words from the Word List that have a similar meaning to these words.
Write the words in sentences in your book. The first one has been done for you.

not dull → *bright* *She wore a bright dress.*

the opposite of 'wrong' →

to struggle fiercely →

a big scare →

the opposite of day →

a difficult situation →

the ability to see →

7 Write as many '**–ight**' words as you can in your book, using the light bulb.
Write some more words of your own.

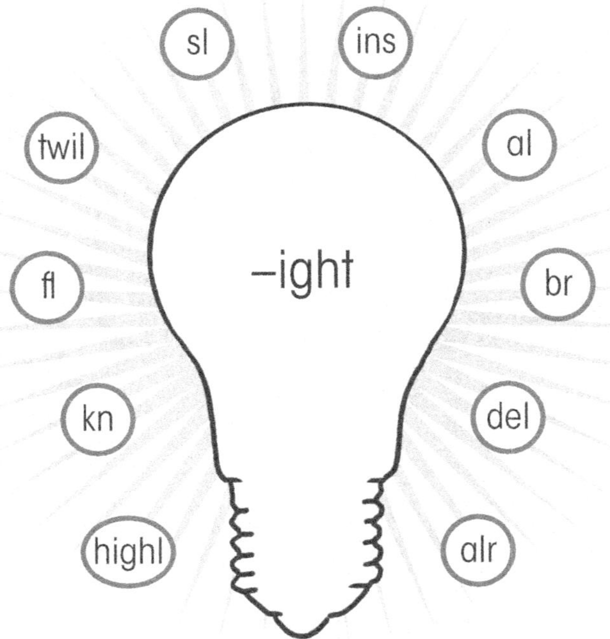

WORD KNOWLEDGE > Verbs

RULE

A **verb** is an **action** word that tells us what someone or something is doing, for example: *run, jump, cry, bark, laugh.*

Verb BOX

put
get
tidy
eat
wave
brush

1 Choose verbs from the Verb Box to fill the gaps. Write the complete sentences in your book.

a. First I _ _ _ out of bed.
b. Next I _ _ _ on my clothes.
c. I know how to _ _ _ _ my room.
d. Mum always tells me to _ _ _ _ _ my hair.
e. I _ _ _ lots of food for breakfast.
f. I give Mum a big hug and _ _ _ _ goodbye.

2 Write the names of three different people or things that could do these actions. The first one has been done for you.

a. sit	*me*	*my dog*	*my grandpa*
b. swim	______	______	______
c. fly	______	______	______
d. sing	______	______	______

COMMON WORDS >

Choose words from the Spelling List to fill the gaps. Write the complete sentence in your book.

1. I caught my _ _ _ _ in the trap.
2. Jonah _ _ _ a new bike for Christmas.
3. We will have to _ _ _ _ _ by three o'clock.
4. Lila left her shoes _ _ _ _ the tree.
5. The teacher said, "You _ _ _ all go home now."

Spelling LIST

got
hand
leave
may
near
bright
sight
right
tight
flight

Writing activity

- Write a description in your book of the things you do on a Sunday morning from the time you get up until lunchtime. Include at least six verbs in your description.

FOCUS > Silent letters 'kn–' 'wr–'

Word BANK

knit wring kneel knuckle trip wrong write knew bank knee

Word LIST

knit
knot
knob
knee
knead
kneel
knew
know
knife
knight
knock
knuckle
wring
wrong
wreck
write
wrote
wrap
wriggle
wrinkle

1 Sort the words from the Word Bank into three groups in your book.

a. words with silent '**kn–**' letters

b. words with silent '**wr–**' letters

c. words with no silent letters

2 There are two words in the Word Bank that do not have a silent letter. Write them in sentences in your book.

3 Choose the correct word. Write the complete sentences in your book.

a. The girl fell over and hurt her (knew / knee).
b. The (knife / knight) was very sharp.
c. At low tide, we can see the (wrap / wreck) of the sailing ship that sank many years ago.
d. Joe will (wrote / write) a letter to his penfriend in Australia.
e. "Do not (wriggle / wrinkle) your pants," said my mother.
f. The policeman will (knock / knot) on every door until he finds the bad boy.
g. The sailor knows how to tie lots of (knits / knots).

4 Write words from the Word List that fit into these word frames.

a. 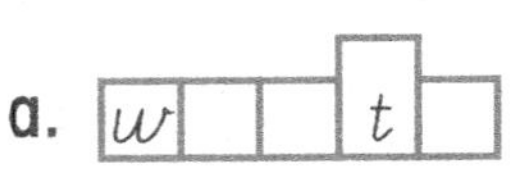

b. 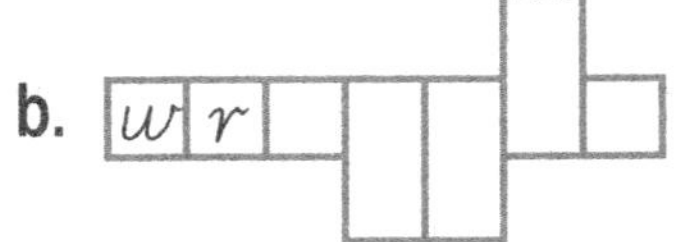

c. 

d. 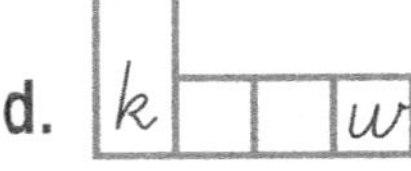

e. 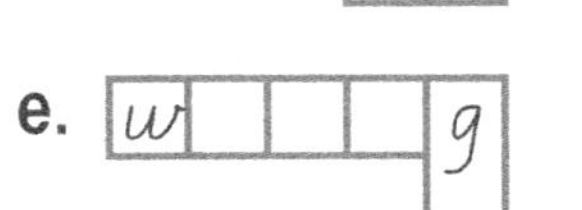

f. 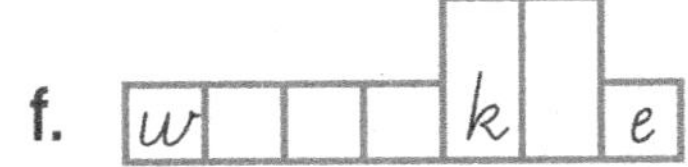

Off the page

■ Draw word frames for these words in your book → knob kneel wring wrote wreck knew

5 Change one letter in each word to make a new word.
Write the new words in sentences in your book. The first one has been done for you.

knit → *knot* *I tied a knot in the string.*

knew → ______ write → ______

6 Find words from the Word List that have a similar meaning to these words.
Write the words in sentences in your book. The first one has been done for you.

part of a leg → *knee* *She fell over and scratched her knee.*

to sit on your knees → *k* _ _ _ _ _ part of a finger → *kn* _ _ _ _ _ _

a tool that cuts things → *k* _ _ _ _ _ a sunken ship → *w* _ _ _ _ _

to cover in paper → *w* _ _ _ to make something from wool → *k* _ _ _

7 Add '–s' to these words to make new words. Write them in sentences in your book.
The first one has been done for you.

I slipped in the mud and fell on my ***knees****.*

knee wriggle wring know knot write knight wrinkle knock

8 Use this code to find words from the Word List. Write the words in your book.

CODE:

k	n	o
i	w	e
g	t	r

a. b.

c. d.

e. f.

9 The last word in each sentence is wrong. Choose a rhyming word from the Word List to replace it. Write the correct sentences in your book.

a. I eat my food with a fork and wife.
b. Will you please turn the door job?
c. It was a very dark fright.
d. She punched the bag with her chuckles.
e. We went out to see the shipneck.
f. Every time I add up the numbers I get them song.

WORD KNOWLEDGE › Present tense verbs

RULE

Remember! **Verbs** are action words.
If an action is happening now, you use the present tense of the verb.
Many present tense verbs end in '**–ing**', for example: I like *jumping* over puddles.

Verb BOX

sniffing
miaowing
flapping
licking
shouting
drinking

1 Choose '**–ing**' verbs from the Verb Box to fill the gaps.
Write the complete sentences in your book.

a. Jenifa is _ _ _ _ _ _ _ an ice block.
b. The dog is _ _ _ _ _ _ _ _ the rubbish.
c. The cat is _ _ _ _ _ _ _ _ because it wants some more milk.
d. The chickens are _ _ _ _ _ _ _ _ their wings.
e. Rina is _ _ _ _ _ _ _ _ soda pop.
f. I can hear Aunty Meri _ _ _ _ _ _ _ _ at the boy.

2 Write these verbs in sentences of your own in your book.

squeaking running eating

COMMON WORDS ›

Spelling LIST

open
play
read
school
than
knife
wrong
know
write
knock

1 Choose words from the Spelling List to fill the gaps.
Write the complete sentences in your book.

a. We like to _ _ _ _ books in class every day.
b. I like going to _ _ _ _ _ _ every day.
c. Eron is older _ _ _ _ my brother.
d. " _ _ _ _ the window to let in some fresh air," said the teacher.
e. We asked our teacher if we could go outside to _ _ _ _ .

2 Write these words in sentences in your book.

wrong knock knife

3 Write the words from the Spelling List in alphabetical order in your book.

Writing activity

- Everybody has jobs to do at home. Write about the jobs you do. Describe what you like doing and what you don't like doing. When you have finished, read your writing. Count how many verbs ending in '**–ing**' you have used.

FOCUS > Silent letters 'l' 'b'

1 Write these words in your book.
Circle the silent letters.

climb calf walk limb hand salmon fork stalk thumb

2 There are two words that do not have a silent letter.
Write them in sentences in your book.

3 Choose the correct word. Write the complete sentences in your book.

a. It was so cold that it made my fingers go (dumb / numb).
b. We (talk / walk) to school every day.
c. A baby cow is called a (palm / calf).
d. The preacher read a (palm / psalm) during the church service.
e. I broke my (crumb / thumb) while playing football.
f. The bird of paradise was sitting on the (limb / lamb) of the tree.
g. A baby sheep is called a (limb / lamb).
h. The time is (talk / half) past three in the afternoon.

4 Write words from the Word List that fit into these word frames.

a. 

b. 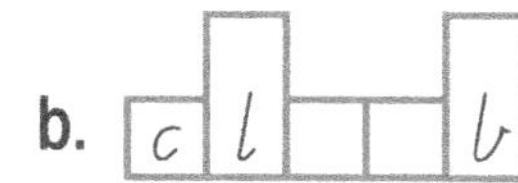

c. 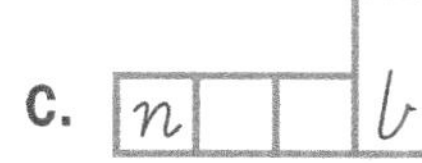

d. 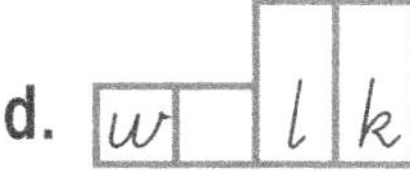

e. 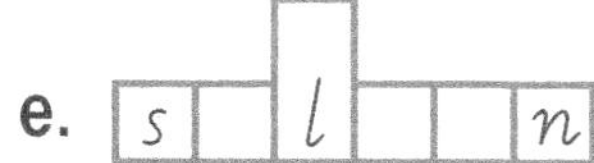

f. 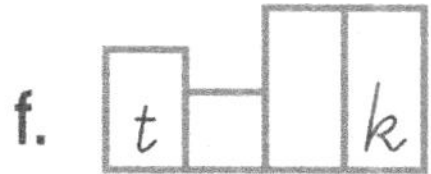

5 Change one letter in each word to make a new word.
Write the new words in sentences in your book. The first one has been done for you.

comb → *bomb* *The bomb went off with a bang.*

limb →

palm →

walk →

yolk →

calf →

dumb →

Word LIST

climb
limb
lamb
comb
crumb
numb
thumb
bomb
dumb
walk
stalk
talk
calm
palm
calf
folk
half
psalm
salmon
yolk

6 Find words from the Word List that have a similar meaning to these words. Write the words in sentences in your book. The first one has been done for you.

quiet and still → *calm* *The sea looks very calm today.*

people → *f* __ __ __

a kind of fish → *s* __ __ __ __ __

a small piece of food → c __ __ __ __

to walk up a steep mountain → *c* __ __ __ __

not clever → *d* __ __ __

to speak → *t* __ __ __

a tree with a large green leaf → *p* __ __ __

a reading in a church service → *p* __ __ __ __

7 Add '–s' to these words to make new words. Write them in sentences in your book. The first one is done for you.

*I went to visit my mother's **folks** on the weekend.*

folk walk crumb limb climb stalk bomb

8 Use this code to find words from the word list. Write the words in your book.

CODE:

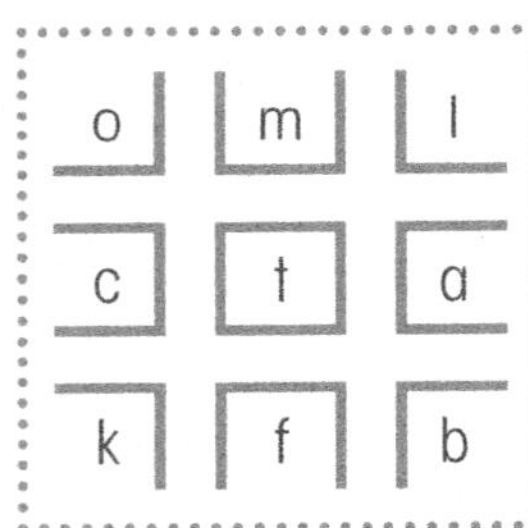

a. ⌐ ┘ ⊔ ⌐

b. ⊓ ┘ L ¬

c. ⊐ ┘ ⊔ ⌐

d. ⊐ ⊏ L ⊓

e. □ ⊏ L ¬

f. L ⊏ ⊔ ⌐

9 The last word in each sentence is wrong. Choose a rhyming word from the word list to replace it. Write the correct sentences in your book.

a. Ana does her hair with a brush and <u>home</u>.

b. Mary had a little <u>ham</u>.

c. That is a good tree to <u>time</u>.

d. We took the dog out for a little <u>cork</u>.

e. The cow had a baby <u>laugh</u>.

f. When Kiri had the injection her mouth went <u>mum</u>.

g. Kiri cut the apple in <u>calf</u>.

WORD KNOWLEDGE > Past tense verbs

RULE

Remember! **Verbs** are action words. If an action has already happened, you use the past tense of the verb. Many past tense verbs end in '**–ed**', for example: I *talked* to my friend.

1 Choose '–ed' verbs from the Verb Box to fill the gaps. Write the complete sentences in your book.

a. The tiger _ _ _ _ _ in the zoo.
b. The dog _ _ _ _ _ _ _ at the cat.
c. The cat _ _ _ _ _ _ its paws.
d. The lion _ _ _ _ _ _ loudly.
e. The dog _ _ _ _ _ _ _ up its dinner.
f. The horse _ _ _ _ _ _ over the fence.
g. Mum _ _ _ _ _ _ _ at the naughty cat.

Verb BOX

lived
roared
gobbled
licked
growled
jumped
shouted

2 Write these verbs in sentences of your own in your book.

opened kicked played helped

COMMON WORDS >

1 Choose words from the Spelling List to fill the gaps. Write the complete sentences in your book.

a. The dog knew its _ _ _ home from the market.
b. We waited _ _ _ _ _ it was dark before we lit the fire.
c. We had to do the exercise _ _ _ _ _ until we got it right.
d. I will _ _ at the post office first thing in the morning to collect the mail.
e. Aaron _ _ _ his homework very quickly.

Spelling LIST

until
way
again
be
did
lamb
bomb
talk
half
walk

2 Write these words in sentences in your book.

walk half talk

3 Write the words from the Spelling List in alphabetical order in your book.

Writing activity

- Imagine if a lion escaped from the zoo. Write about what might have happened. Use plenty of past tense verbs.

FOCUS > 'y' '–ight' and silent letters

1 Write words in your book to keep the patterns going.
The first one has been done for you.

a.	pry	fly	shy	why	sty	dry
b.	flight	knight	sight	______	______	______
c.	wring	wrong	wreck	______	______	______
d.	climb	lamb	thumb	______	______	______
e.	knob	knee	know	______	______	______
f.	chalk	stalk	talk	______	______	______

2 Choose the correct word. Write the complete sentences in your book.

a. Jimi tried to (climb / crumb) the coconut tree.
b. Pia (knew / know) that she should not take the necklace.
c. Laena went to bed late last (fright / night).
d. We will (talk / walk) to school this morning.
e. Arno saw the snake (wrinkle / wriggle) through the grass.
f. Uncle Kiva's shoes were too (tight / right).
g. You must (fly / fry) the egg before you eat it.

3 Find words for the pictures. Write them in your book.

4 Find the odd word out in each line. Write it in a sentence in your book.

a.	by	my	pry	sigh	try	why
b.	climb	bomb	lamb	bone	thumb	numb
c.	stalk	walk	calf	cow	half	palm
d.	fight	might	sight	fright	kit	night

5 Write as many words as you can in your book, using the magic word machines.

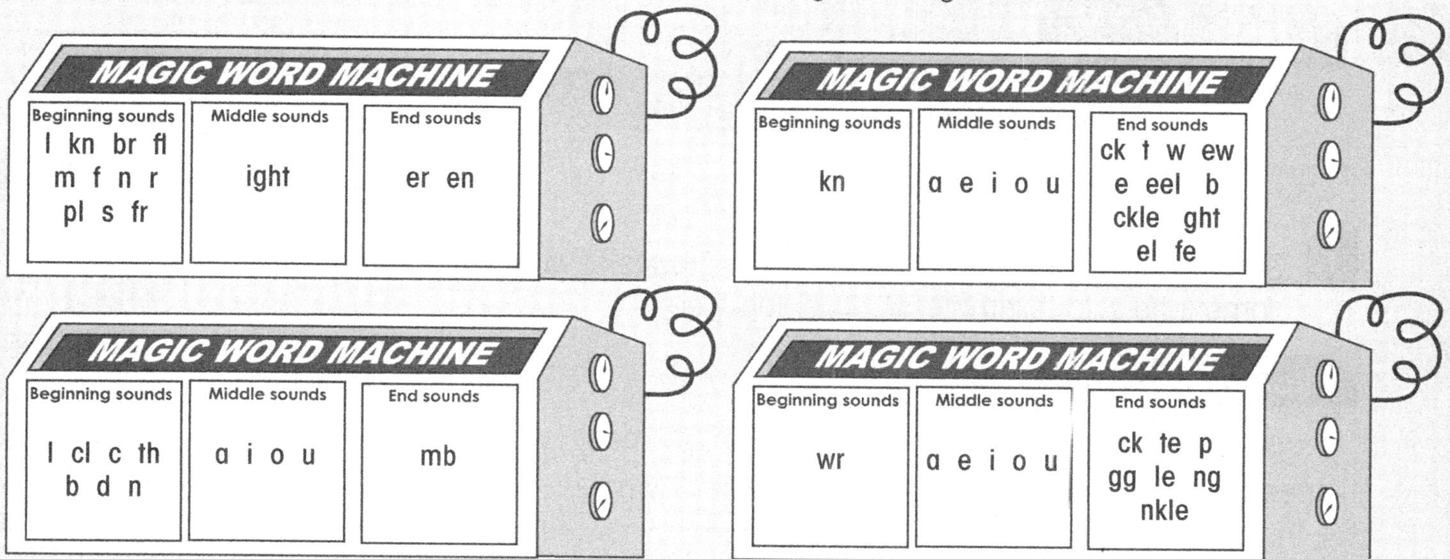

6 Fill in the missing letters to make the words in these puzzles. Write them in your book.

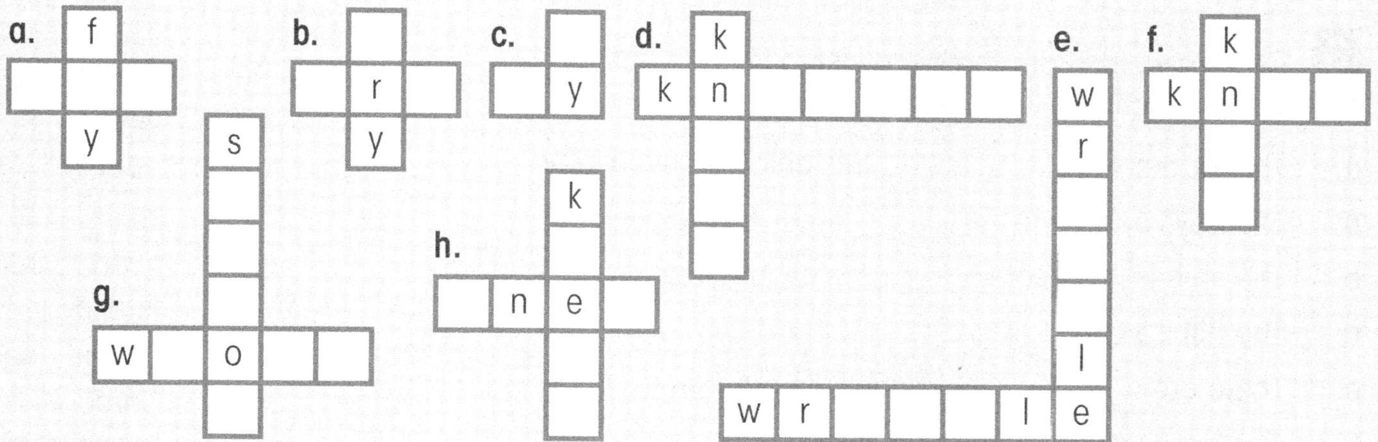

7 Each brick in the wall contains a word that follows the one before, with just one new letter. Use the clues to find the missing words and write them in your book. The first row of bricks has been done for you.

round handle on door *knob*	to find out *know*	the past tense of know *knew*	the middle part of a leg *knee*
very clever *sly*	to see something	a pig's home	to go high in the air
correct, not wrong *right*	when it is dark	the power to see	fits very closely
to make with needles *knit*	a twist in a piece of rope	the present tense of knew	a round handle on a door
to go up in the air *fly*	to cook in a pan	to shed tears	not wet

Unit 21

FOCUS › 'ee' words

1 Sort the words from the Word Bank into groups of words that end with the same letters, for example: sleep, creep, weep.

Word BANK

teeth street greed queen greet weep bee week sleep heel
speed green free peek creep sweet wheel screen tree

2 Choose three words from the Word Bank.
Write them in sentences in your book.

3 Choose words from the Word List to fill the gaps.
Write the complete sentences in your book.

a. The farmer will _ _ _ _ his chickens every day.
b. The boys agreed to _ _ _ _ at 12 o'clock.
c. The ship is made of _ _ _ _ _.
d. The hill is very _ _ _ _ _.
e. There are _ _ _ _ _ boys in our family.
f. Our family goes to church every _ _ _ _.
g. The boy was _ _ _ _ downtown near the market.
h. We need to _ _ _ _ the garden before we plant new crops.
i. "You are late! Where have you _ _ _ _"?

Word LIST

sweep	cheek
sheep	week
creep	seek
steep	creek
sleep	feet
keep	sheet
deep	greet
weep	fleet
bleep	meet
jeep	street
tree	sweet
three	peel
free	feel
bee	steel
see	heel
feed	reel
bleed	wheel
speed	seen
weed	screen
need	queen
seed	green
greed	keen
breed	been
peek	

RHYME time › Copy this rhyme into your book and then ...

Underline the words ending in '**–eet**'.

Tweet, tweet.
Girl on street
Waits to meet
Someone sweet.

Tweet, tweet.
Bird on street
Waits to greet
Someone sweet.

Girl… street
Bird… greet
Both… meet
That's… sweet.

4 Find words from the Word List that have a similar meaning to these words. Write the words in sentences in your book. The first one has been done for you.

an army truck → *jeep* *The jeep has very thick tyres.*

to cry a lot →	a colour →
the back part of a foot →	a part of a face →
a plant grows from this →	a group of ships →

5 Find the odd word out in each line. Write it in a sentence in your book.

a.	meet	green	meat	weep	seed
b.	week	greet	weak	bleep	keep
c.	bee	sea	queen	see	speed
d.	need	creek	free	creak	sleep
e.	feet	reel	eel	real	need
f.	steep	bleed	sweat	wheel	breed

6 Use this code breaker to find the missing words. Write the words in your book in complete sentences.

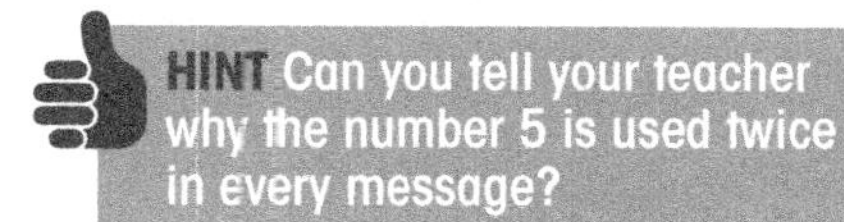
HINT Can you tell your teacher why the number 5 is used twice in every message?

a	b	c	d	e	f	g	h	i	j	k	l	m	n	o	p	q	r	s	t	u	v	w	x	y	z
1	2	3	4	5	6	7	8	9	10	11	12	13	14	15	16	17	18	19	20	21	22	23	24	25	26

a. (3, 18, 5, 5, 11)
b. (7, 18, 5, 5, 4)
c. (16, 5, 5, 11)
d. (7, 18, 5, 5, 20)
e. (23, 8, 5, 5, 12)
f. (19, 3, 18, 5, 5, 14)

7 Change one letter in each word to make a new word. Write the new words in your book. The first one has been done for you.

peek → *peel*	seek → ______	keep → ______	greet → ______
seed → ______	bee → ______	feel → ______	greed → ______
week → ______	sheet → ______	sleep → ______	weep → ______
tree → ______	green → ______	cheek → ______	beet → ______
feel → ______	been → ______	preen → ______	

WORD KNOWLEDGE › Syllables

RULE

Words can be broken down into **syllables**. Syllables help us to say and spell a word.
Every syllable has a **vowel sound** or a '**y**' in it.
Some words have one syllable: *car, truck, cat.*
Some words have two syllables: *pen/cil, wat/er, ci/ty.*
Some words have three syllables: *po/ta/to, ba/na/na, croc/o/dile.*
Some words have four syllables: *cass/o/wa/ry, therm/om/et/er, ant/i/sep/tic.*

1 Copy these words into your book. Divide the words into syllables with one vowel sound in each syllable. The first one has been done for you.

a.	grass	*grass*	b.	but	______
	hopper	*hop/per*		butter	______
	grasshopper	*grass/hop/per*		butterfly	______
c.	fish	______	d.	king	______
	fisher	______		kingfish	______
	fisherman	______		kingfisher	______

COMMON WORDS ›

1 Choose words from the Spelling List to fill the gaps.
Write the complete sentence in your book.

a. The mountain was very _ _ _ _ and difficult to climb.
b. The boy promised _ _ _ _ _ to be late home again.
c. Most people write with their _ _ _ _ _ hand.
d. The hungry man wanted _ _ _ _ food.
e. May I go to town _ _ _ _ _ _ ?

2 Write these words in sentences in your book.

speed wheel weak

3 Write the words from the Spelling List in alphabetical order in your book.

Weekly Spelling List to be tested at the end of the week

Spelling LIST

high
more
never
please
right
jeep
speed
week
sweet
wheel

Writing activity

- What happens to the rubbish at your school? Make a list of things that the students could do to make your school a cleaner place.

FOCUS > 'ea' words

Word LIST

weak
speak
beak
leak
lean
mean
clean
bean
cream
steam
dream
scream
feast
beast
east
least
seat
beat
neat
meat
heat
peach
beach
teach
reach

1 Sort the words from the Word Bank into groups of words that end with the same letters, for example: seat, neat, beat.

Word BANK

teeth cream mean eagle neat scream speak beat
leaf beak lean clean please weak dream seat

2 Choose words from the Word List to fill the gaps. Write the complete sentences in your book.

- **a.** The bird's __ __ __ __ was very sharp.
- **b.** We heard the baby __ __ __ __ __ __ when she fell over.
- **c.** I had a bad __ __ __ __ __ when I went to sleep.
- **d.** She sat on a __ __ __ __ that was broken.
- **e.** We went for a swim at the __ __ __ __ __.
- **f.** Boiling water makes lots of __ __ __ __ __.
- **g.** Close the lid so that the milk won't __ __ __ __ from the bottle.
- **h.** I will __ __ __ __ __ you how to spell that word.
- **i.** She can __ __ __ __ you in a race any time.

RHYME time > Copy this rhyme into your book and then ...

1. Underline the '**ea**' words.
2. Say the rhyme quietly to yourself then say it out loud with the class.

I scream, you scream,
We all scream
for ice cream.

I dream, you dream,
We all dream
of ice cream.

So…
if I scream
and you dream,

Let's give
the whole team
some ICE CREAM!

3 Find words from the Word List that have a similar meaning to these words. Write the words in sentences in your book. The first one has been done for you.

to talk → *speak* *I will speak to you tomorrow.*

something to sit on → ______ very tidy → ______

nasty → ______ not dirty → ______

a juicy fruit → ______ not strong → ______

4 Write words from the Word List that fit into these word frames.

a. *l* ___ b. *p* ___ c. *l* ___ d. *p* ___ e. *w* ___

5 Find the odd word out in each line. Write it in a sentence in your book.

a.	meat	seat	creep	beat	heat
b.	cream	dream	stream	seem	steam
c.	lean	mean	clean	learn	bean
d.	feast	east	best	least	beast
e.	teach	peach	each	beef	reach
f.	week	speak	bead	leak	beak

6 Use this code breaker to find the missing words. Write the words in your book in complete sentences.

a	b	c	d	e	f	g	h	i	j	k	l	m	n	o	p	q	r	s	t	u	v	w	x	y	z
1	2	3	4	5	6	7	8	9	10	11	12	13	14	15	16	17	18	19	20	21	22	23	24	25	26

a. (16, 12, 5, 1, 19, 5)
b. (23, 5, 1, 11)
c. (19, 3, 18, 5, 1, 13)
d. (6, 5, 1, 19, 20)
e. (4, 18, 5, 1, 13)
f. (5, 1, 7, 12, 5)

7 Change one letter in each word to make a new word. Write the new words in your book. The first one has been done for you.

beak → *leak* feast → ______ beach → ______ meat → ______

lean → ______ seat → ______ teach → ______ least → ______

WORD KNOWLEDGE > Syllables

RULE

Remember! Words can be broken down into **syllables**. Syllables help us to say and spell a word. Every syllable has a vowel sound or a '**y**' in it, for example: *po/ta/to*.

Look at the pictures of the animals. Write their names in your book.
Divide the words into syllables with one vowel sound in each syllable.
Write how many syllables are in each word. The first one has been done for you.

caterpillar *cat/er/pill/ar* 4	grasshopper	pig	eagle
butterfly	kingfisher	cockatoo	possum

COMMON WORDS >

1 Choose words from the Spelling List to fill the gaps.
Write the complete sentence in your book.

a. My first _ _ _ _ is Simon.
b. I was _ _ _ when my pet died.
c. You _ _ _ _ to like that book.
d. My sister ate a big _ _ _ of cake.
e. Although Jona was little, he won the _ _ _ _.

Spelling LIST

- seem
- name
- bit
- race
- sad
- ice cream
- clean
- please
- reach
- speak

2 The word 'ice cream' is made of two words – 'ice' and 'cream'.
Break these words into two parts. Write a sentence for each part in your book.

necklace grandfather airport

3 Write the words from the Spelling List in alphabetical order in your book.

Writing activity

- Do you think it would be good if you could eat ice cream every day?
Write some reasons for your answer.

FOCUS › '–ow' words (as in 'grow')

Word LIST

show
low
blow
bow
flow
slow
glow
grow
row
snow
tow
crow
own
know
yellow
window
arrow
below
tomorrow
borrow
rainbow
pillow
elbow
bellow
burrow

1 Use the Word List to help write these words in full. Write them in your book.

a. __ho__ b. __ro__ c. __lo__ d. __lo__
e. __ro__ f. __ __ __ lo__ g. __no__ h. b__l__w
i. __lo__ j. __ __ bow k. __ __ __ ro__

2 Choose words from the Word List to fill the gaps.
Write the complete sentences in your book.

a. The opposite of high is __ __ __.
b. He shot the bird with an __ __ __ __ __.
c. If you are too __ __ __ __, you will never get there.
d. Open the __ __ __ __ __ __ and let some air in.
e. Our visitors are coming the day after __ __ __ __ __ __ __ __.

3 Find words from the Word List that have a similar meaning to these words.
Write the words in sentences in your book. The first one has been done for you.

not quick → *slow* *He was so slow he came last.*
to make a sound like a rooster → ______
a colour → ______
white flakes that fall from the sky → ______
to get bigger → ______
something you lie your head on → ______
to pull something along → ______

RHYME time › Copy this rhyme into your book and then ...

1. Underline the '**–ow**' words.
2. Say the rhyme and do the actions.

Eenie meenie miney mo,
Who would like to have a go?
First, walk fast…
Now, walk slow…
Then, stretch high…

Now, crouch low…
Around the room, away you go!
Faster walk,
Now s—l—o—w.

Now high, now low,
STAND STILL.
Down you go!
Walk fast,
Crouch low!

4 Write words from the Word List that fit into these word frames.

a. 
s

b. r

c. 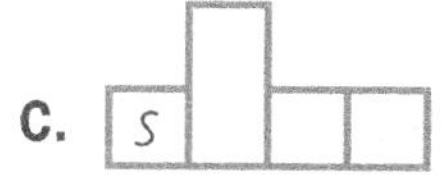
s

d. 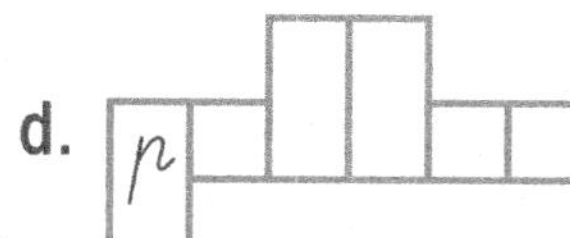
p

e. 
e

f. r

g. b

h. t

5 Find the odd word out in each line. Write it in a sentence in your book.

a.	low	elbow	slow	beach	below
b.	tomorrow	know	yesterday	own	row
c.	row	grow	pillow	sheet	snow
d.	slow	mow	grow	go	tow
e.	tow	below	elbow	tow	above
f.	grow	groan	tow	know	slow

6 Use this code breaker to find the missing words.
Write the words in your book in complete sentences.

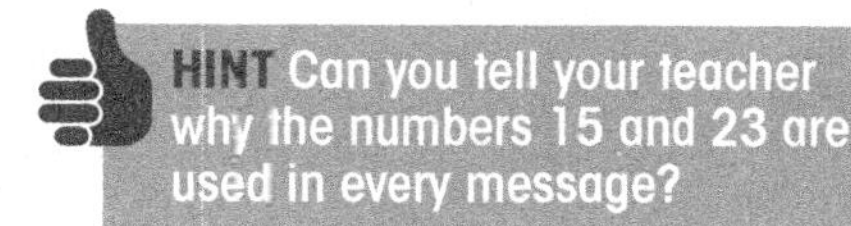
HINT Can you tell your teacher why the numbers 15 and 23 are used in every message?

a	b	c	d	e	f	g	h	i	j	k	l	m	n	o	p	q	r	s	t	u	v	w	x	y	z
1	2	3	4	5	6	7	8	9	10	11	12	13	14	15	16	17	18	19	20	21	22	23	24	25	26

a. (7, 18, 15, 23)

b. (1, 18, 18, 15, 23)

c. (11, 14, 15, 23)

d. (23, 9, 14, 4, 15, 23)

e. (2, 15, 18, 18, 15, 23)

f. (18, 15, 23)

g. (20, 15, 23)

h. (20, 15, 13, 15, 18, 18, 15, 23)

7 Change one letter in each word to make a new word. Write the new words in your book.
The first one has been done for you.

low → bow　　grow → ______　　bellow → ______

slow → ______　　row → ______　　burrow → ______

WORD KNOWLEDGE > Alphabetical order

1 Find words for these ten pictures. Write them in alphabetical order in your book. One word has been done for you.

a ____
b ____
c ____
d ____
e agle
f ____
g ____
h ____
i ____
j ____

2 Write these words in your book in alphabetical order.

mango letter necklace oil rice paddle sage toea up worm
girl fish market learn net old picture sad touch us wall

HINT
Be careful! You might have to look at the second letter in a word to get the right order.

COMMON WORDS >

1 Choose words from the Spelling List to fill the gaps. Write the complete sentence in your book.

a. We _ _ _ _ _ the lost dog in the bush.
b. Do you think you will _ _ _ _ to be one hundred?
c. I like to read a _ _ _ _ at night.
d. Dad gets up early in the _ _ _ _ _ _ _.
e. My sister and I _ _ _ _ go to school.

2 Write these words in sentences in your book.

show own below

3 Write the words from the Spelling List in alphabetical order in your book.

Spelling LIST

book
both
found
live
morning
below
know
show
own
grow

Writing activity

- How do you make a headdress for a sing sing? Describe what you need and how you make it. Draw some pictures to go with your instructions.

Unit 24

FOCUS > 'oa' words

1 Use the Word List to write these words in full. Write them in your bock.

b__ __t   s__ __p   m__ __n   t__ __ __ __t   l__ __ __

g__ __t   c__ __ __   __ __ts   r__ __d

2 Choose words from the Word List to fill the gaps.
Write the complete sentences in your book.

a. We use __ __ __ __ when we wash our hands.
b. There was a big pot hole in the __ __ __ __ .
c. The truck had a large __ __ __ __ of coconuts.
d. At the end of the game, the __ __ __ __ __ talked to the team.
e. Mum bought a __ __ __ __ of bread for lunch today.
f. The boy let out a __ __ __ __ when he was hit by the ball.
g. We need to find a __ __ __ __ to cross the river.
h. Lia's sore __ __ __ __ __ __ __ made her cough a lot.
i. I like to eat __ __ __ __ __ for breakfast.

Word LIST

boat
coat
goat
moat
oats
float
throat
road
load
foam
groan
loan
soap
loaf
toast
boast
coach
moan

3 Write words from the Word List that fit into these word frames.

a. 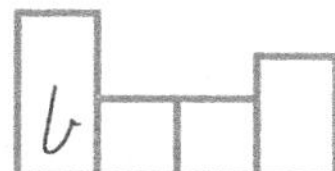
b. f
c. l
d. b
e. r
f. 

RHYME time > Copy this rhyme into your book and then …

Underline the '**–oat**' words.

The goats
got on the boat
to cross the moat
to eat the oats
on the other side of the hill.

BUT …
the goats didn't get there.
Why?
Because the boat didn't float!

4 Find words from the Word List that have a similar meaning to these words. Write the words in sentences in your book. The first one has been done for you.

it floats on water → *boat* *They rowed the boat to the bank of the river.*

it has horns and hoofs → ______

food goes down it to your stomach → ______

you wear it to keep warm → ______

you wash yourself with it → ______

to stay on top of the water → ______

a sound like a groan → ______

5 Build new words by adding **'–s'**, **'–ed'** and **'–ing'** to these base words. Write the new words in your book. The first one is done for you.

a. coat → *coats coating coated*

b. float **c.** load **d.** foam **e.** groan

f. toast **g.** boast **h.** moan

6 Write these words in sentences in your book.

float floats floating floated

7 Use this code breaker to find the missing words. Write the words in your book in complete sentences.

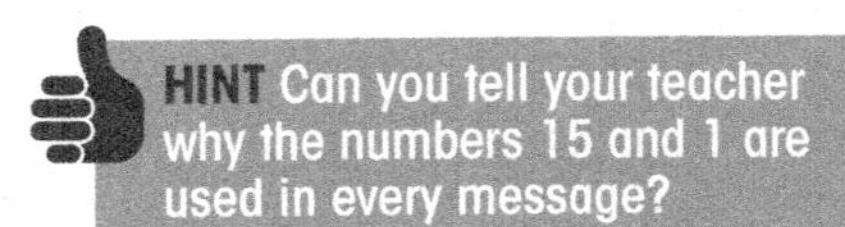

a	b	c	d	e	f	g	h	i	j	k	l	m	n	o	p	q	r	s	t	u	v	w	x	y	z
1	2	3	4	5	6	7	8	9	10	11	12	13	14	15	16	17	18	19	20	21	22	23	24	25	26

a. (18, 15, 1, 4)

b. (3, 15, 1, 3, 8)

c. (19, 15, 1, 16)

d. (20, 8, 18, 15, 1, 20)

e. (6, 15, 1, 13)

f. (15, 1, 20, 19)

8 Change one letter in each word to make a new word. Write the new words in your book. The first one has been done for you.

goat → *coat* moan → ______ loan → ______

road → ______ boast → ______ roam → ______

WORD KNOWLEDGE > Alphabetical order

Draw this brick wall in your book. Put words from the Word List in alphabetical order to fill in the bricks. Write the words in your book. The first and last words have been done for you.

boast				
			toast	

COMMON WORDS >

1 Choose words from the Spelling List to fill the gaps. Write the complete sentence in your book.

a. Can I come ____ to your place?

b. We gave our teacher a _______ for his birthday.

c. Dad came home late last _____.

2 Write these words in sentences in your book.

day shall coat soap

3 Write the words from the Spelling List in alphabetical order in your book.

Weekly Spelling List to be tested at the end of the week

Spelling LIST

night
over
present
shall
day
coat
road
groan
coach
soap

Writing activity

- Write a story in your book about goats. Don't forget to include a beginning, a middle and an end.

Revision

FOCUS › 'ee', 'ea', '–ow', 'oa' words

1 Write words in your book to keep the patterns going. The first one has been done for you.

a.	sheep	creep	deep	*peep*	*seep*	*steep*
b.	meat	wheat	heat	______	______	______
c.	low	blow	slow	______	______	______
d.	goat	moat	float	______	______	______
e.	greed	bleed	seed	______	______	______
f.	stream	beam	cream	______	______	______

2 Choose the correct word. Write the complete sentences in your book.

a. The boys tried to (row / blow) the boat across the river.
b. The burnt (foam / toast) tasted horrible.
c. We saw the monkey climb the (bee / tree).
d. Can you (steel / peel) this orange for me?
e. Mum tried to (peach / teach) the baby to walk.
f. I am too (week / weak) to lift the rock.
g. We always have (meat / meet) for our dinner.
h. The old black (grow / crow) flew from the tree.

3 Find the odd word out in each line. Write it in a sentence in your book.

a.	snow	crow	row	tow	groan	grow
b.	goat	moat	float	road	coat	throat
c.	seat	heat	meat	neat	beat	meet
d.	feed	bleed	seed	creek	greed	need
e.	keep	sheep	sheet	jeep	peep	weep

4 Change one letter in each of these words to make a new word. Write the new words in your book. The first one has been done for you.

row → *tow*	bellow → ______	boast → ______	poach → ______
reach → ______	dream → ______	beat → ______	least → ______
willow → ______	road → ______	row → ______	peek → ______
seen → ______	slow → ______	coats → ______	

5 Write as many words as you can in your book, using the magic word machines.

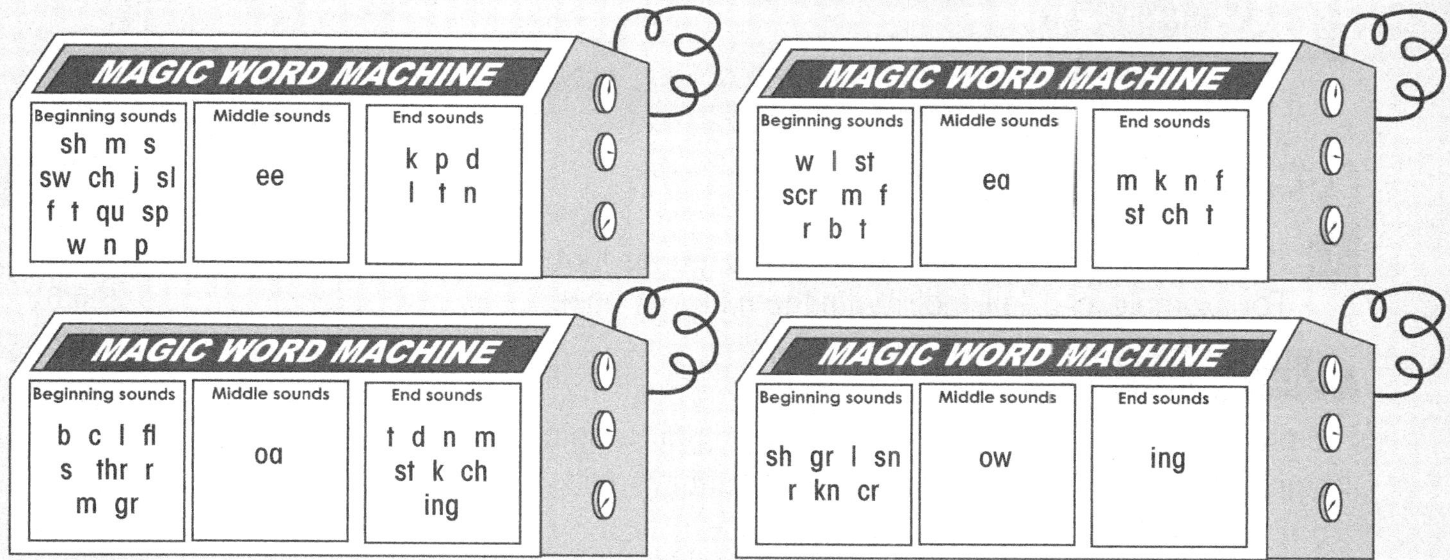

6 Build new words by adding '–s', '–ed' and '–ing' to these base words.
Write the new words in your book. The first one has been done for you.

a. tow → *tows towed towing*

b. seed **c.** coat **d.** greet **e.** steam **f.** row

7 Each brick in the wall contains a word that follows the one before, with just one new letter.
Use the clues to find the missing words and write them in your book.
The first row of bricks has been done for you.

to grab *reach*	a stone fruit *peach*	to help to learn *teach*	the seaside *beach*
to put seeds in ground *sow*	not high	what a boat does	to pull along
to take a look *peep*	to cry	a small military car	not shallow
an action *deed*	to give food	to want something	a tiny plant

Unit 26

FOCUS › 'ai' words

1 Sort the words from the Word Bank into groups that end with the same letters. For example: p<u>ail</u>, f<u>ail</u>, m<u>ail</u>. Write them in your book.

Word BANK

teeth train plain main hail chain pail maid paid
paint grain fail mail stain faint afraid laid

2 Choose three words from the Word Bank.
Write each one in a sentence in your book.

3 Choose words from the Word List to fill the gaps.
Write the complete sentences in your book.

a. They had to use a _ _ _ _ _ to pull the car out of the mud.
b. I was _ _ _ _ _ _ when the dog growled at me.
c. The _ _ _ _ _ pulled in to the platform.
d. Get a _ _ _ _ of water to put out the fire.
e. We need some _ _ _ _ if we are going fishing.
f. My mother could not wash the _ _ _ _ _ from my shirt.
g. The cat screeched when I stood on its _ _ _ _.
h. I saw the ship _ _ _ _ into the bay.
i. We helped the teacher to _ _ _ _ _ the walls of our classroom.
j. I _ _ _ _ a lot of money to get my bike fixed.

Word LIST

train
main
pain
again
stain
grain
chain
brain
plain
rail
tail
pail
mail
sail
fail
wail
hail
paint
faint
wait
bait
paid
maid
laid
afraid

RHYME time › Copy this rhyme into your book and then …

Underline three words ending with '**–ain**'.

There was a young lady of Spain
Who was dreadfully sick on a train.
Not once, but again
And again and again
And again
And again
And again!

4 Find words from the Word List that have a similar meaning to these words. Write the words in sentences in your book. The first one has been done for you.

an ache or hurt → *pain* *I had a stomach pain.*

used to make things colourful → ______ icy rain → ______

the postman delivers it → ______ to be frightened → ______

to stay → ______ you use it to think → ______

5 Write words from the Word List that fit into these word frames.

a.  b. 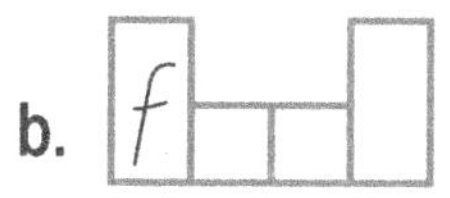 c. 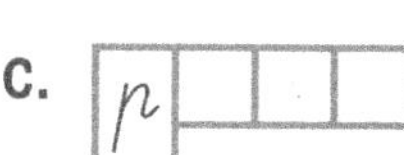

d. 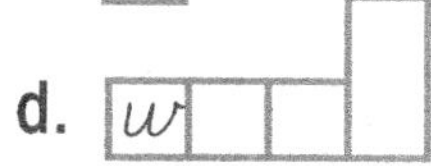 e.  f. 

6 Find the odd word out in each line. Write it in a sentence in your book.

a.	paid	maid	paint	afraid	laid
b.	pail	mail	sale	sail	tail
c.	pain	maid	main	again	stain
d.	nail	snail	rail	gale	bail
e.	train	faint	tram	rain	brain

7 Use this code breaker to find the missing words. Write the words in your book in complete sentences.

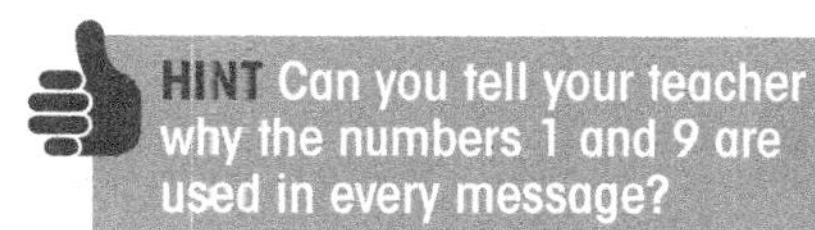

a	b	c	d	e	f	g	h	i	j	k	l	m	n	o	p	q	r	s	t	u	v	w	x	y	z
1	2	3	4	5	6	7	8	9	10	11	12	13	14	15	16	17	18	19	20	21	22	23	24	25	26

a. (3, 8, 1, 9, 14)
b. (23, 1, 9, 20)
c. (16, 1, 9, 14, 20)
d. (1, 6, 18, 1, 9, 4)
e. (19, 20, 1, 9, 14)
f. (20, 1, 9, 12)

8 Change one letter in each word to make a new word. Write the new words in your book. The first one has been done for you.

pain → *main* rail → ______ paid → ______ grain → ______

paint → ______ bait → ______ rail → ______

WORD KNOWLEDGE › Compound words

RULE

Compound words are made when two words are joined to make a bigger word.
For example: *rail + way = railway, hail + storm = hailstorm.*

1 Join these words together to make compound words.
Write the complete words in your book.

in + to = ____________ break + fast = ____________

sun + shine = ____________ foot + ball = ____________

2 Find a compound word from the Compound Word Box to match these clues.
Write the words in your book.

a. You mother's mother or father's mother
b. A big spiky fruit
c. A kind of nut
d. Your teacher uses chalk on it
e. You store cups and plates in it
f. Your mother's father or father's father
g. It goes around your neck
h. A kind of boat

Compound Word BOX

necklace
outrigger
grandma
grandpa
cupboard
chalkboard
pineapple
peanut

COMMON WORDS ›

1 Choose words from the Spelling List to fill the gaps.
Write the complete sentences in your book.

a. Open the window and let in some fresh _ _ _.
b. Go inside and _ _ _ _ _ _ those dirty shorts!
c. Do you have _ _ _ more chocolates?
d. A _ _ _ _ _ big coconut fell on me.
e. My teacher said I was very _ _ _ _ today.

2 Write these words in sentences in your book. paint brain sail paid

3 Write the words from the Spelling List in alphabetical order in your book.

Spelling LIST

great
good
air
any
change
brain
sail
paint
paid
afraid

■ When was the last time that you were really afraid? Write and draw what happened.

FOCUS > '–ay' words

1 Use the Word List to write these words in full. Write them in your book.

s__a__ | S__ __d__ __ | r__l__y
y__s__ __r__a__ | sl__ __ | p__ __ __
r__ __w__y | F__ __d__ __ | b__ __ __h__ __y
__e__n__s__a__ | r__y

2 Choose words from the Word List to fill the gaps.
Write the complete sentences in your book.

a. Can you come to __ __ __ __ at my place tomorrow?
b. A __ __ __ of sun came shining through the trees.
c. Some people go to church on __ __ __ __ __ __.
d. The plane took off from the __ __ __ __ __ __.
e. The day after Tuesday is __ __ __ __ __ __ __ __ __.
f. Horses and cows eat __ __ __.
g. The ship sailed into the __ __ __.
h. It is my tenth __ __ __ __ __ __ __ __ tomorrow
i. Our team won the 400 metres __ __ __ __ __ race yesterday.

Word LIST

say
pay
may
pray
stay
play
bay
clay
hay
ray
slay
today
yesterday
birthday
Monday
Tuesday
Wednesday
Thursday
Friday
Saturday
Sunday
runway
relay

RHYME time > Copy this rhyme into your book and then ...

1. Underline the words that end with '**–ay**'.
2. Find a word where the '**–e**' make the '**a**' say its own name. Write it in a sentence in your book.

Old Johnny Ray
One holiday
Thought he would go
For a swim in the bay

A shark at play
Came that way
Oh, what a shame
Poor old Johnny Ray!

3 Find words from the Word List that have a similar meaning to these words. Write the words in sentences in your book. The first one has been done for you.

don't go → *stay* *I want to stay home today.*

dried grass → ______

to give someone money in return for work → ______

a beam of sunlight → ______

this day → ______

to say holy words → ______

the day before this day → ______

4 Write words from the Word List that fit into these word frames.

a. 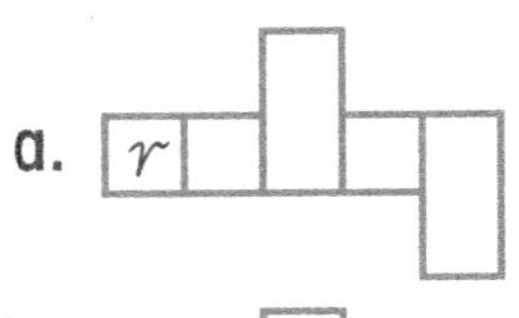

b. r

c. 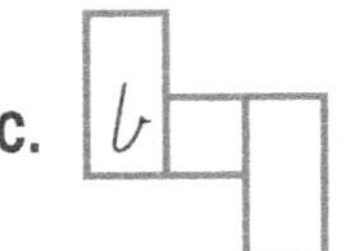

d. 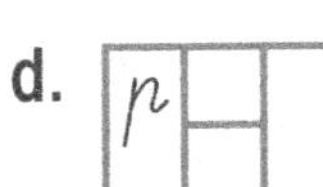

e. 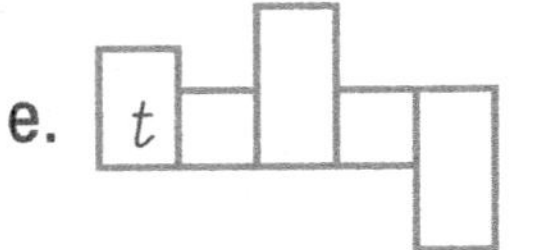

f. 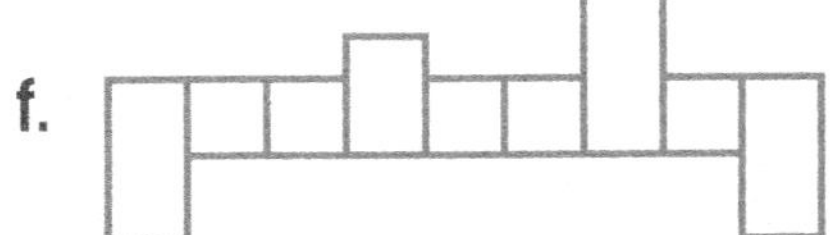

g. 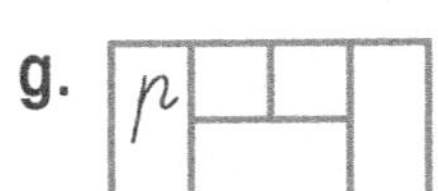

5 Find the odd word out in each line. Write it in a sentence in your book.

a.	bay	say	may	train	day
b.	Sunday	birthday	Tuesday	yesterday	weekend
c.	relay	byway	hooray	steak	highway
d.	slay	today	payday	holiday	yesterday
e.	great	day	bay	slay	dray
f.	today	yesterday	Monday	May	June

6 Use this code breaker to find the missing words. Write the words in your book in complete sentences.

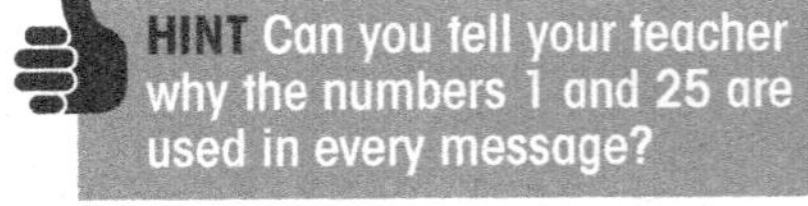
HINT Can you tell your teacher why the numbers 1 and 25 are used in every message?

a	b	c	d	e	f	g	h	i	j	k	l	m	n	o	p	q	r	s	t	u	v	w	x	y	z
1	2	3	4	5	6	7	8	9	10	11	12	13	14	15	16	17	18	19	20	21	22	23	24	25	26

a. (19, 20, 1, 25)

b. (18, 21, 14, 23, 1, 25)

c. (19, 12, 1, 25)

d. (18, 5, 12, 1, 25)

7 Change one letter in each word to make a new word. Write the new words in your book. The first one has been done for you.

say → *may*

slay → ______

delay → ______

pay → ______

fray → ______

clay → ______

WORD KNOWLEDGE > Compound words

✱ RULE

Remember! **Compound words** are made when two smaller words are joined to make a bigger word. For example: *birth* + *day* = *birthday*.

1 Use the sun to make compound words beginning with '**sun–**'. Write them in your book. The first one has been done for you.

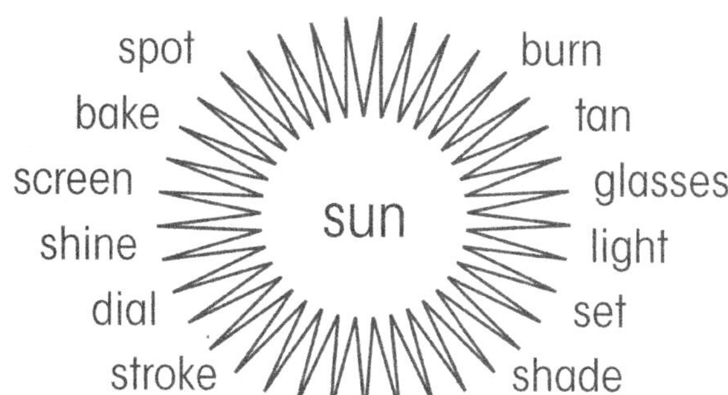

sun + shine = sunshine

____

____

____

____

____

2 Write four compound words that begin with '**play–**' in your book.

3 Break these compound words into two parts. Write each part in a sentence in your book.

sunbake basketball

COMMON WORDS >

1 Choose words from the Spelling List to fill the gaps. Write the complete sentences in your book.

a. I like a drink of _ _ _ _ _ after playing sport.

b. His mother said, "Come inside _ _ _ !"

c. She came _ _ _ _ _ in the 100 metres race.

d. The worm dug deep _ _ _ _ into the soil.

e. Have you seen _ _ bike anywhere?

Weekly Spelling List to be tested at the end of the week

Spelling LIST

my
water
down
first
now
birthday
stay
today
may
play

2 Write these words in sentences in your book.

today stay birthday

3 Write the words from the Spelling List in alphabetical order in your book.

Writing activity

- Write a story about your birthday. What would you do if it was your birthday and you could do anything you liked?

FOCUS > 'oi' words

Word LIST

oil
boil
coil
foil
spoil
coin
join
point
joint
moist
noise
choice
voice
toil
hoist
broil
rejoice
coiled
boiled

1 Sort the words from the Word Bank into groups that end with the same letters. For example: jo<u>int</u>, po<u>int</u>. Write them in your book.

Word BANK

boil joint coil coin oil rejoice point
moist spoil join voice choice foil

2 Choose three words from the Word Bank. Write each one in a sentence in your book.

3 Choose words from the Word List to fill the gaps. Write the complete sentences in your book.

a. We use coconut _ _ _ for cooking.
b. The snake _ _ _ _ _ _ _ around the rim of the wheel.
c. They will _ _ _ _ _ the flag up high when they win.
d. If you put too much water in the soup, you will _ _ _ _ _ it.
e. I needed a _ _ _ _ to buy a lolly.
f. I lost my _ _ _ _ _ when I had a sore throat.
g. There was trouble because the children made too much _ _ _ _ _.
h. You should _ _ _ _ the water before you make the tea.
i. We are going to _ _ _ _ the club before next season.

RHYME time > Copy this rhyme into your book and then ...

1. Underline the '**oi**' words.
2. Write them in sentences in your book.

Mary had a little lamb,
She fed it castor oil.
And everywhere the lamb would go,
It fertilized the soil!

4 Find the odd word out in each line. Write it in a sentence in your book.

a.	boil	oil	foil	boy	spoil
b.	boiled	joined	spoiled	spike	toilet
c.	join	point	moist	trail	coil
d.	oiling	spoiling	boiling	staying	toiling
e.	choice	poise	nice	join	foil

5 Write words from the Word List that fit into these word frames.

a. 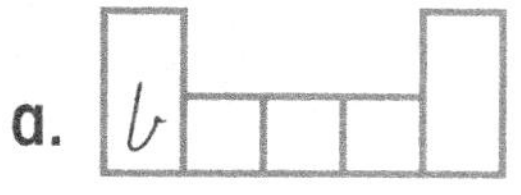

b. p

c. j

d. c

e. o

f. b

6 Build new words by adding '**–s**', '**–ed**' and '**–ing**' to these words.
Write the new words in your book. The first one is done for you.

a. oil → *oils oiled oiling*

b. foil c. boil d. join e. point f. coil

7 Find words from the Word List that have a similar meaning to these words.
Write the words in sentences in your book. The first one has been done for you.

to make very hot → *boil You must boil the water to make tea.*

to damage or ruin →

a twist in a rope →

the sharp end of something →

a small amount of money →

damp →

you use this for talking →

8 Use this code breaker to find the missing words.
Write the words in your book in complete sentences.

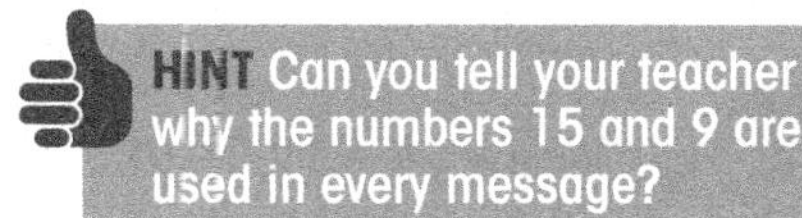

HINT Can you tell your teacher why the numbers 15 and 9 are used in every message?

a	b	c	d	e	f	g	h	i	j	k	l	m	n	o	p	q	r	s	t	u	v	w	x	y	z
1	2	3	4	5	6	7	8	9	10	11	12	13	14	15	16	17	18	19	20	21	22	23	24	25	26

a. (3, 15, 9, 14)

b. (15, 9, 12)

c. (19, 16, 15, 9, 12)

d. (10, 15, 9, 14)

e. (14, 15, 9, 19, 5)

f. (18, 5, 10, 15, 9, 3, 5)

WORD KNOWLEDGE > Contractions

✱ RULE

Contractions are where **two** words make **one** word.
We use an **apostrophe** to show where a letter is left out, for example: *we + are = we're.*

1 Read the words below. Choose contractions from the Contraction Box to match the words. Write these contractions in sentences in your book. The first one has been done for you.

he is → he's → *He's going to school tomorrow.*

they are → we have → it is → must not →

you are → they have → did not →

Contraction BOX

didn't
it's
they're
you're
he's
we've
mustn't
they've

2 Write these sentences in your book. Circle the contractions.

a. I can't run today.
b. It's going to be very hot.
c. He's a silly boy.
d. Don't touch the chocolates.
e. I didn't do it.
f. I think we're finished now.
g. Let's sit down to eat.

COMMON WORDS >

1 Choose words from the Spelling List to fill the gaps. Write the complete sentences in your book.

a. Make sure you _ _ _ _ _ a note to school today.
b. Do you think you _ _ _ _ _ swim that river?
c. He climbed the _ _ _ _ to get the coconuts.
d. I cannot _ _ _ _ _ where I put my book.
e. The sun went behind the _ _ _ _ _ fluffy clouds.

2 Write these words in sentences in your book. boiled voice spoil

3 Write the words from the Spelling List in alphabetical order in your book.

Spelling LIST

think
tree
white
bring
could
spoil
join
noise
boiled
voice

RHYME time > Copy this rhyme into your book and then ...

Circle the contractions then write them in full in your book.

I've got a dog as thin as a rail
He's got fleas all over his tail.
Every time his tail goes flop
The fleas on the bottom all hop to the top.

Unit 29

FOCUS > 'oy' words

1 Use the Word List to write these words in full. Write them in your book.

j__ __ t__ __s en__ __ __ em__ __ __ __
an__ __y oys__ __ __ b__ __ j__y__ __l r__ __al

2 Choose words from the Word List to fill the gaps.
Write the complete sentences in your book.

a. I need a new battery for the __ __ __ train.

b. A new __ __ __ came to our school today.

c. If you __ __ __ __ __ the teacher you will get into trouble.

d. It is a long __ __ __ __ __ __ from Rabaul to Port Moresby by boat.

e. The school is going to __ __ __ __ __ __ a new cleaner.

f. I hope you will __ __ __ __ __ the meal I cooked for you.

g. The __ __ __ __ __ __ I ate tasted really bad.

h. I hope I will get lots of __ __ __ __ for my birthday.

Word LIST

boy
joy
enjoy
toy
employ
destroy
annoy
royal
loyal
oyster
enjoy
toys
employing
voyage
joyful
coy

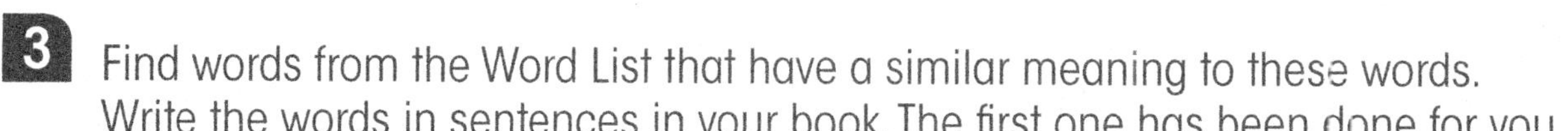

3 Find words from the Word List that have a similar meaning to these words.
Write the words in sentences in your book. The first one has been done for you.

faithful → *loyal* *Michael is a fond and loyal friend to me.*

to make angry →

a journey →

to feel happy and glad →

to ruin something →

a young male →

to give someone a job →

RHYME time > Copy this rhyme into your book and then …

1. Underline the words that end with '**–oy**'.
2. How many words with a capital '**B**' did you find?

Boy over the water,
Boy over the sea,
Boy broke the toy boat
And blamed it on me.

Boy told ma,
Ma told pa,
Boy got into trouble,
Ha, ha, ha.

4 Write words from the Word List that fit into these word frames.

a. a
b. e
c. b
d. r
e. t
f. l
g. v
h. j
i. c

5 Find the odd word out in each line. Write it in a sentence in your book.

a.	joy	boy	toy	soy	blow
b.	annoys	finger	boys	joy	boy
c.	joyful	noisy	loyal	enjoy	voyage
d.	enjoying	annoying	girls	destroying	employing
e.	royal	loyal	coin	toy	coy
f.	annoy	voice	enjoys	annoyed	annoying

6 Use this code breaker to find the missing words. Write the words in your book in complete sentences.

HINT Can you tell your teacher why the numbers 15 and 25 are used in every message?

a	b	c	d	e	f	g	h	i	j	k	l	m	n	o	p	q	r	s	t	u	v	w	x	y	z
1	2	3	4	5	6	7	8	9	10	11	12	13	14	15	16	17	18	19	20	21	22	23	24	25	26

a. (18, 15, 25, 1, 12)
b. (12, 15, 25, 1, 12)
c. (10, 15, 25)
d. (3, 15, 25)
e. (2, 15, 25)
f. (5, 14, 10, 15, 25, 5, 4)
g. (5, 13, 16, 12, 15, 25, 9, 14, 7)

7 Find the words in these puzzles. Write them in your book.

a.
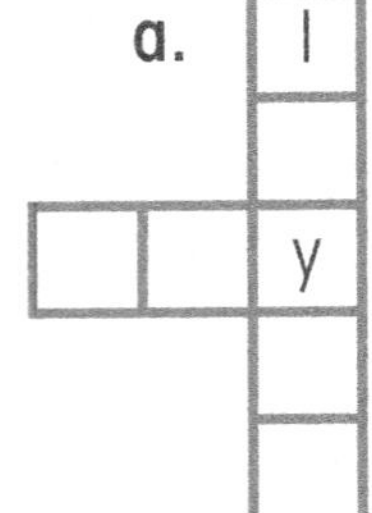

b.
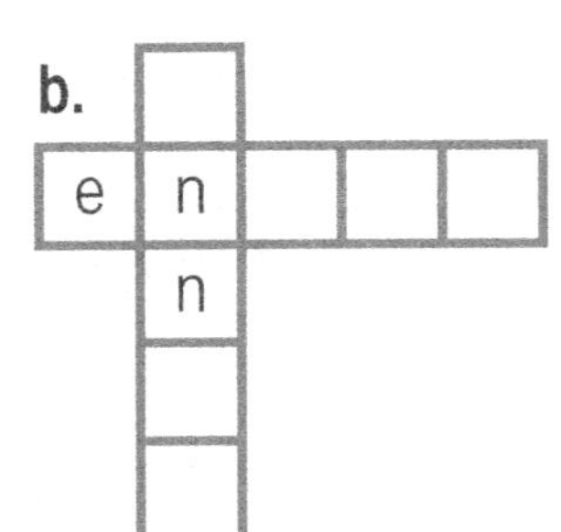

c.

d.
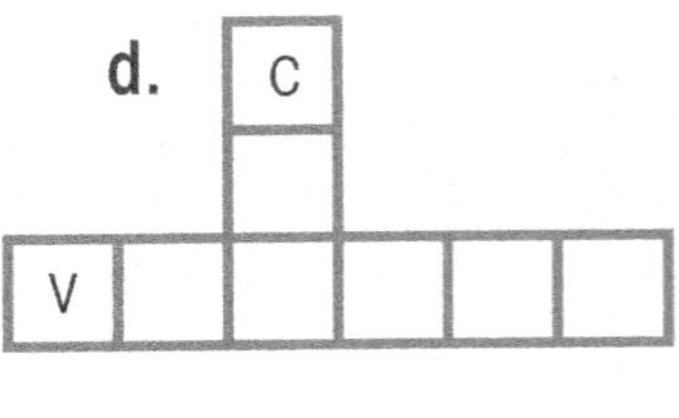

WORD KNOWLEDGE > Contractions

RULE

Remember! **Contractions** are where **two** words make **one** word.
We use an **apostrophe** to show where a letter is left out, for example: *it* + *is* = *it's*.

1 Do the word sums below. Replace the bold letter with an apostrophe, then write the contraction in a sentence in your book. The first one has been done for you.

she + **i**s = *she's* → *She's using the computer now.*

I + **a**m = is + n**o**t = we + **a**re =

did + n**o**t = let + **u**s =

2 Write the contractions in full in your book. Then write them in sentences in your book. The first one has been done for you.

a. I'm *I am going to the movies tomorrow.*

b. it's

c. we've

d. you're

e. I've

COMMON WORDS >

1 Choose words from the Spelling List to fill the gaps. Write the complete sentences in your book.

a. We have _ _ _ _ fingers on each hand.
b. John said, "This work is _ _ _ hard."
c. Lai's _ _ _ _ _ _ made her lunch for her.
d. We locked the _ _ _ _ _ when we went out.
e. "We will be there _ _ _ _," said the bus driver.

2 Write these words in sentences in your book.

oyster enjoy loyal

3 Write the words from the Spelling List in alphabetical order in your book.

Writing activity

- Write about a time when you were lost or left alone.
  Write about what happened and how you felt. Use some contractions in your writing.

Spelling LIST

five
house
mother
soon
too
enjoy
toy
boy
loyal
oyster

FOCUS › 'ai', '-ay', 'oi', 'oy' words

1 Write words in your book to keep the patterns going. The first one has been done for you.

a.	pain	main	chain	gain	train	drain
b.	say	may	pray	______	______	______
c.	oil	boil	coil	______	______	______
d.	enjoy	annoy	boy	______	______	______
e.	Monday	Tuesday	Wednesday	______	______	______
f.	toys	destroys	enjoys	______	______	______

2 Choose the correct word. Write the complete sentences in your book.

a. We all (enjoyed / annoyed) the big feast at the market.
b. The parents decided to (faint / paint) the school.
c. You must (boil / spoil) the water before you cook the egg.
d. This fire will (enjoy / destroy) the forest.
e. It was a long (voyage / employ) to Port Moresby.
f. I could see the rat's (mail / tail) sticking out of the hole.
g. Can I go out to (say / play) now?
h. The juice made a (pain / stain) on his shirt.

3 Find the odd word out in each line. Write it in a sentence in your book.

a.	coy	joy	boy	draw	toy	soy
b.	Monday	Wednesday	July	Friday	Sunday	Tuesday
c.	pail	mail	fail	tail	stray	hail
d.	coin	point	joint	loyal	join	points
e.	stain	grain	great	brain	plain	main

4 Change one letter in each of these words to make a new word.
Write the new words in your book. The first one has been done for you.

royal → loyal   grain → ______   hoist → ______   toys → ______

laid → ______   boil → ______   paint → ______   slay → ______

wait → ______   slaying → ______

5 Write as many words as you can in your book, using the magic word machine.

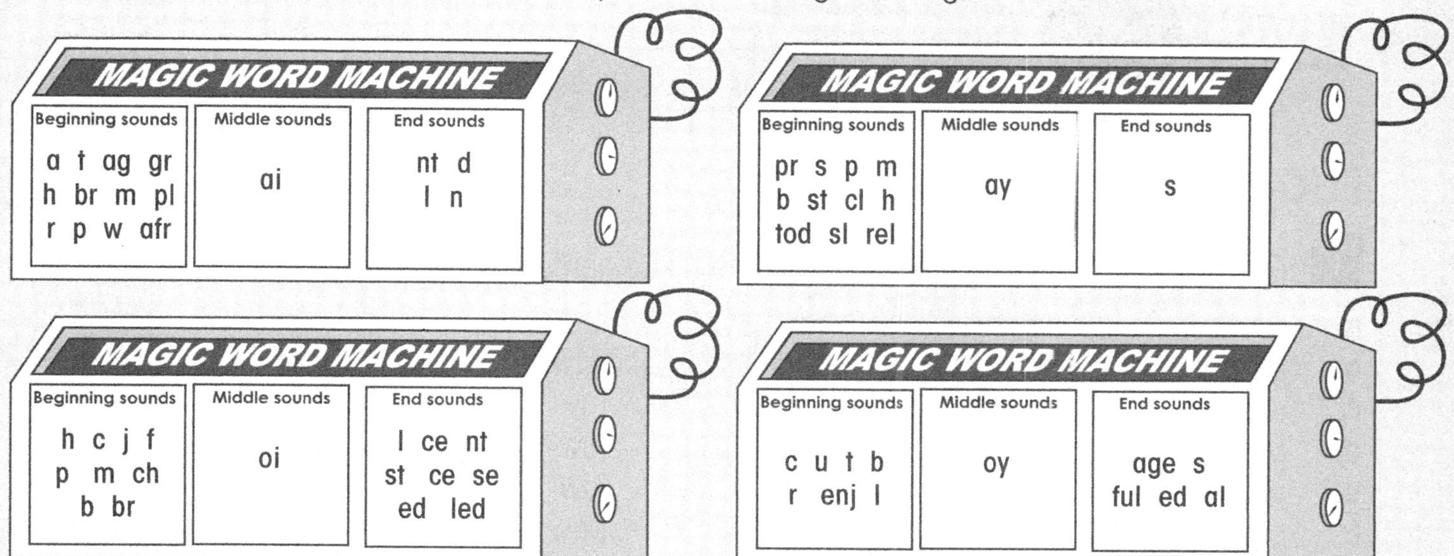

6 Build new words by adding '–s', '–ed' and '–ing' to these words.
Write the new words in your book. The first one has been done for you.

a. annoy → *annoys annoyed annoying*

b. enjoy **c.** sail **d.** spoil **e.** boil **f.** stay

7 Each brick in the wall contains a word that follows the one before, with just one new letter.
Use the clues to find the missing words and write them in your book.
The first row of bricks has been done for you.

the back part of an animal *tail*	letters and parcels *mail*	a bucket *pail*	to get some money *paid*
to stop someone *foil*	to make very hot	to twist around	small metal money
to get rid of water *drain*	you think with it	it moves on rails	a seed that grows
a kind of bean *soy*	a young male	something to play with	shy or dreamy
a female servant *maid*	to get money for work	a bucket	to not be able to do something

Unit 31

FOCUS > 'aw' words

1 Find the odd word out in each line. Write it in a sentence in your book.

a.	paw	squaw	how	straw
b.	jigsaw	paws	giant	flaw
c.	seesaw	outlaw	flow	raw
d.	pray	pawpaw	gnaw	jaw
e.	paw	jump	raw	jaw
f.	saw	raw	floor	paw

2 Find words from the Word List that have a similar meaning to these words. Write the words in sentences in your book. The first one has been done for you.

a nail on an animal's paw → *claw*

The parrot used its claw to pick up seeds from the ground.

to make a picture →

not cooked →

a bone in your head →

an animal's foot →

you use this in a playground →

you use this to cut down trees →

you use this to drink with →

a large fruit →

3 Write words from the Word List that fit into these word frames.

a. c _ _ _

b. p _ _ _

c. p _ _ _ _ _

d. g _ _ _

e. s _ _ _ _

f. j _ _ _ _ _

g. s _ _ _ _ _

h. o _ _ _ _ _

Word LIST

caw
claw
draw
flaw
gnaw
jaw
law
paw
raw
saw
squaw
straw
thaw
chainsaw
jigsaw
outlaw
pawpaw
seesaw
sawdust
strawberry
drawer

RHYME time > Copy this rhyme into your book and then …

1. Underline the words that end with '**–aw**'.
2. Write three of those words in sentences in your book.

I saw a paw,
An ENORMOUS paw.
At the end of the paw
Was a pointy claw,

And above the claw
Was a mighty jaw,
And out of that jaw
Came a VERY LOUD ROAR! So I ran!

4 Use the beginning sounds to write '**–aw**' words.
Write the words in alphabetical order in your book.

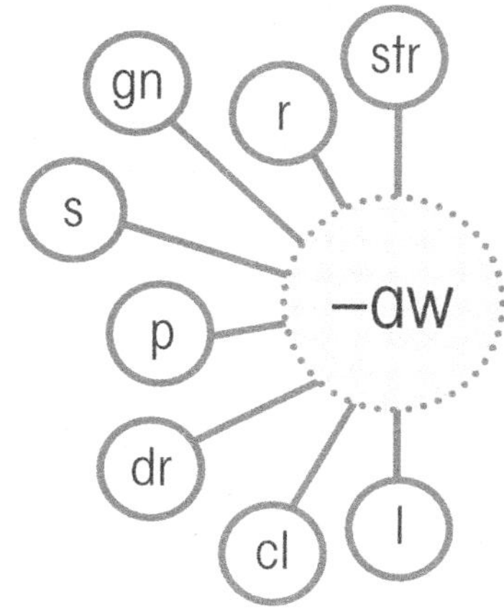

5 Choose words from the Word List to fill the gaps.
Write the complete sentences in your book.

a. Our cat has a sore _ _ _.
b. The artist will help us to _ _ _ _ a picture of a cuscus.
c. A female American Indian is called a _ _ _ _ _.
d. It is fun to drink from a bottle with a _ _ _ _ _.
e. The farmer used a _ _ _ _ _ _ _ _ to cut up the large logs.
f. We have many _ _ _ _ _ _ trees in our garden.

6 These words are written backwards.
Change them around to make '**–aw**' words from the Word List.
Write them in your book.

war → was → ward →
warts → reward →

7 The last word in these sentences is wrong.
Find a rhyming word that fits then write the complete sentence in your book.
The first one has been done for you.

a. The bird grabbed its prey with its <u>sore</u>. *The bird grabbed its prey with its claw.*
b. The lion likes to eat its meat <u>poor</u>.
c. We drank our drink with a <u>door</u>.
d. I like to ride on the <u>jigsaw</u>.

WORD KNOWLEDGE > Adverbs

RULE

Adverbs tell **how** something is done. They often end in '**–ly**'.
They are placed before or after the verb, for example: *slowly, softly, carefully*.
Think of 'adverb' as 'add + verb'. It will add to what you know about the verb.

1 Write these sentences in your book.
Draw a circle around the adverbs in each sentence.

a. The children are talking loudly in the classroom
b. Leti whispered softly to her friend.
c. The sun shone brightly.
d. The car had a puncture and it stopped suddenly.
e. Paul swam quickly across the river.
f. Jenifa walked slowly along the bush track.

2 Complete these sentences with an interesting adverb. Write the sentences in your book.

a. Uncle Sam spoke ___________.
b. The leaf fell ___________.
c. The naughty boy shouted ___________.
d. The boat sank ___________.
e. The sun shone ___________.

COMMON WORDS >

1 Choose words from the Spelling List to fill the gaps.
Write the complete sentences in your book.

a. Simon asked the teacher _ _ _ we had to go.
b. My _ _ _ _ _ _ and I went into the village.
c. It is _ _ _ _ a long way to the river.
d. I kicked the _ _ _ _ over the fence.
e. We had to _ _ _ _ _ still for twenty minutes.

2 Write these words in sentences in your book.

pawpaw claw draw

3 Write the words from the Spelling List in alphabetical order in your book.

Spelling LIST

why
ball
friend
stand
such
thaw
claw
pawpaw
draw
jaw

Writing activity

- Imagine you are teaching someone to fish. Write about how to catch a fish.
Describe the equipment you would need and the important things you must do.

FOCUS > 'ew' words

1 Find the odd word out in each line. Write it in a sentence in your book.

a.	dew	flew	fish	flew
b.	jewel	diamond	pew	blew
c.	threw	new	stand	brew
d.	blew	knew	crew	know
e.	letter	corkscrew	grew	chew
f.	stew	soup	flew	grew

2 Find words from the Word List that have a similar meaning to these words. Write the words in sentences in your book.
The first one has been done for you.

not many → *few* *There are only a few fish left in the pond.*

cooked meat with vegetables → ______ not old → ______

tossed away → ______ became bigger → ______

a precious stone → ______ tiny drops of water on grass → ______

to munch food with teeth → ______ it removes corks → ______

Word LIST

dew
few
knew
grew
new
pew
blew
brew
chew
crew
drew
flew
screw
stew
threw
jewel
corkscrew

3 Write words from the Word List that fit into these word frames.

a. *b* □□□ b. *t* □□□□ c. *j* □□□□

d. *s* □□□□ e. *s* □□□ f. *n* □□ g. *d* □□□

4 Change one letter in each word to make a new word.
Write the new words in sentences in your book.

few → *new* → *I have a new toy.*

a. brew → ______ b. chew → ______ c. blew → ______

! Challenge

■ Find a word from the Word List with a silent 'k'. Write it in a sentence in your book.

5 Use the beginning sounds to write '–ew' words.
Write the words in alphabetical order in your book.

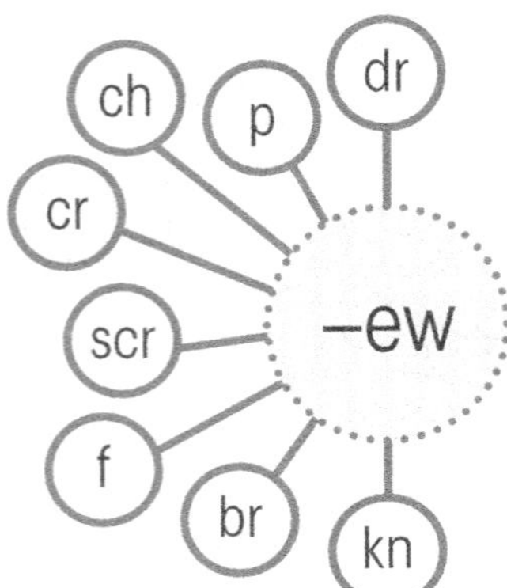

6 Choose words from the Word List to fill the gaps.
Write the complete sentences in your book.

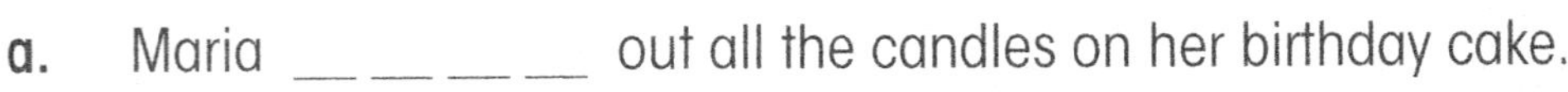

a. Maria _ _ _ _ out all the candles on her birthday cake.
b. Grandma will _ _ _ _ _ the lid tightly on the bottle.
c. We are going to have a fish _ _ _ _ for dinner tonight.
d. The bird _ _ _ _ from her nest.
e. The chief _ _ _ _ a circle on the map.
f. They needed a _ _ _ _ _ _ _ _ _ to open the bottle of wine.
g. Pia's hair _ _ _ _ very long before she had it cut.
h. In the early morning, the _ _ _ was still on the grass.

7 Choose the correct word. Write the complete sentences in your book.

a. The villagers (know / knew) the right track to take.
b. Leti (grew / grow) six centimetres this year.
c. When I said three, she (blow / blew) the candles out.
d. Dad (threw / throw) the ball to Simon.
e. Kari (draw / drew) the picture for her aunty.

8 Use this code to find words from the Word List. Write the words in your book.

CODE:

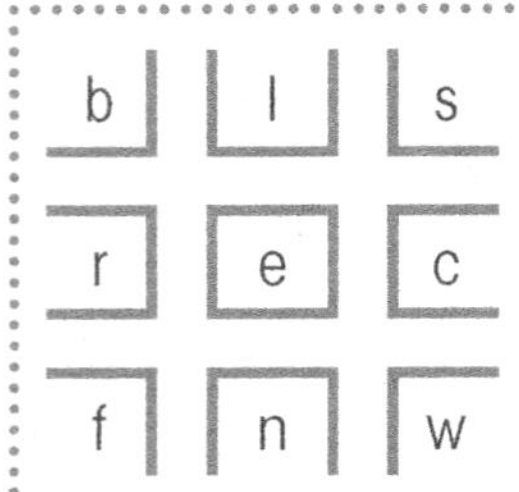

a.

b.

c.

d.

e.

f.

g.

WORD KNOWLEDGE > Adverbs

RULE

Remember! Adverbs tell **how** something is done. They often end in '**–ly**'.
They are placed before or after the verb, for example: *slowly, softly, carefully*.

1 Choose the best adverb to complete each sentence.
Write the complete sentences in your book.

a. Aunty Meri held the baby bird (gently / tightly).
b. Uncle Sam snored (loudly / carefully).
c. Simon ran home (heavily / quickly).
d. Pia played in her bedroom (slowly / quietly).
e. Sam gobbled his food (greedily / politely).

2 Write sentences in your book with these adverbs.

heavily smoothly loudly

COMMON WORDS >

1 Choose words from the Spelling List to fill the gaps.
Write the complete sentences in your book.

a. Are you _ _ _ _ you want to go to the market today?
b. Letti has _ _ _ _ _ eyes and black hair.
c. I used my bilum to _ _ _ _ _ the fruit home.
d. We walked _ _ _ _ _ the track until we came to the village.
e. When I blow out the candles on the cake, I will _ _ _ _ for something special.

2 Write these words in sentences in your book. knew flew grew

3 Write the words from the Spelling List in alphabetical order in your book.

Writing activity

- Write some instructions for a friend to follow. For example, 'Jump three times, nod your head, spin around, sit down, clap your hands and walk to the door'. Use adverbs to tell them how to follow the instructions. For example, 'Jump lightly three times and nod your head slowly'. Brainstorm some more adverbs you could use before you start. Swap your instructions with a friend.

Weekly Spelling List to be tested at the end of the week

Spelling LIST

sure
wish
along
brown
carry
flew
knew
new
grew
jewel

Unit 33

FOCUS › 'ow' words (as in 'cow')

Word LIST

cow
now
how
brown
clown
crowd
prowl
growl
flower
shower
powder
owl
down
crown
town
gown
howl
tower
drown
towel
somehow
anyhow
eyebrow
power

1 Find the odd word out in each line. Write it in a sentence in your book.

a.	down	how	towel	brush
b.	somehow	eyebrow	anywhere	anyhow
c.	growl	prowl	roar	howl
d.	flower	power	shadow	shower
e.	gown	sandals	frown	down
f.	owls	cows	lions	fowls

2 Find words from the Word List that have a similar meaning to these words. Write the words in sentences in your book. The first one has been done for you.

to cry out loud → *howl* *The baby let out a howl.*

a circus performer → ______ a lot of people in one place → ______

this animal gives us milk → ______ a part of a plant → ______

you use it to dry yourself → ______ a period of light rain → ______

3 Write words from the Word List that fit into these word frames.

a. 
b. 
c. g

d. 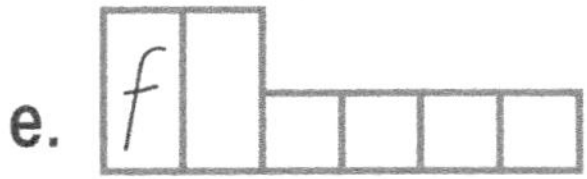
e. 
f. o

4 Change one letter in each word to make a new word.
Write the new words in sentences in your book.
The first one has been done for you.

prowl → *growl* → *I heard the dog growl.*

a. gown → b. tower → c. cow → d. crown →

Off the page

■ Join these small words together to make compound words, for example: *some* + *how* = *somehow*.
any + how gun + powder eye + brow sun + flower sun + shower

5 Use the beginning and end sounds to write '**–ow**' words as in 'cow'.
Write the words in alphabetical order in your book. The first one has been done for you.

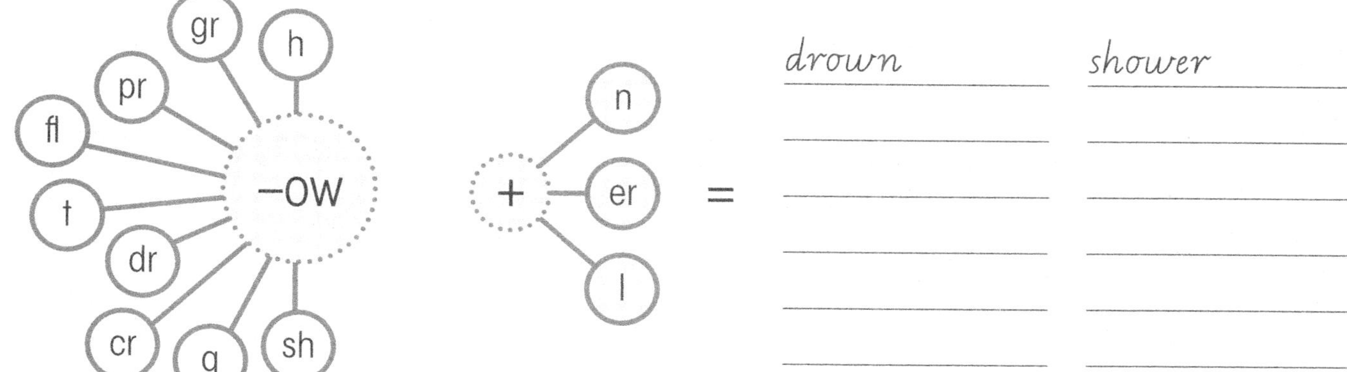

6 Choose words from the Word List to fill the gaps.
Write the complete sentences in your book.

a. There was a big __ __ __ __ __ at the market today.

b. The large __ __ __ made a strange hooting sound.

c. The tall building had a high __ __ __ __ __.

d. The dog began to __ __ __ __ __ when the stranger came near.

e. The circus __ __ __ __ __ made everyone laugh.

f. Don't forget your __ __ __ __ __ when you come swimming today.

7 Find words from the Word List in this word search puzzle.
Write them in your book.

p	o	w	l	s	h	o	w	e	r
x	c	r	o	w	d	e	t	c	h
e	y	e	b	r	o	w	n	o	w
s	v	g	o	w	n	d	o	w	n
e	m	s	o	m	e	h	o	w	b
n	o	w	l	z	q	h	o	w	l

8 Use this code to find words from the Word List. Write the words in your book.

CODE:

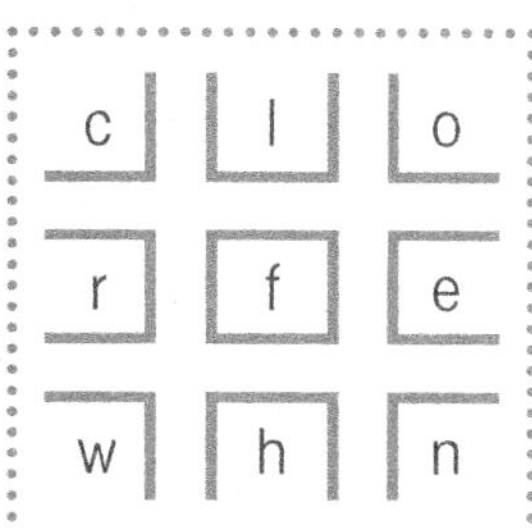

a. ┘ └ ┐

b. ⊓ └ ┐

c. ┘ ⊔ └ ┐ ┌

d. └ ┐ ⊔

e ┌ └ ┐

f. □ ⊐ └ ┐ ┌

g. □ ⊔ └ ┐ ⊏ ⊐

h. ┘ ⊐ └ ┐ ┌

WORD KNOWLEDGE › Prepositions

RULE

A **preposition** tells where something is, for example: *in, on, under, around, with.*
The cat is <u>in</u> the tree. The preposition is 'in'.

1 Choose a preposition from the Preposition Box to complete each sentence. Write the complete sentences in your book.

a. The car sped _ _ _ _ _ the road.
b. The arrow went _ _ _ _ _ _ _ the target.
c. The little boy sat _ _ _ _ _ _ his mother.
d. The people stepped _ _ _ _ the bus.
e. The rabbit crawled _ _ _ _ its burrow.
f. The man jumped _ _ _ _ the hurdle.

Preposition BOX

through
onto
over
along
beside
into

2 Write sentences in your book with these prepositions.

in under with around

COMMON WORDS ›

1 Choose words from the Spelling List to fill the gaps. Write the complete sentences in your book.

a. The small boy _ _ _ under the table.
b. I fell _ _ _ _ and hurt my knee.
c. Petra found an _ _ _ _ way through the bush.
d. Aunty Grace _ _ _ _ us all some cakes.
e. I scratched my _ _ _ _ when I ran through the trees.

Spelling LIST

didn't
easy
face
gave
hid
crowd
flower
down
somehow
power

2 Write these words in sentences in your book.

somehow power didn't

3 Write the words from the Spelling List in alphabetical order in your book.

Writing activity

- What would you do if you were lost in the bush? What might you do to get safely home?

Unit 34

FOCUS > 'oo' words (as in 'moon')

Word LIST

moon
soon
room
noon
root
hoot
boot
shoot
cool
pool
roof
spoon
brood
broom
balloon
food
mood
boot
tooth
goose
loose
bedroom
zoom
kangaroo

1 Find the odd word out in each line. Write it in a sentence in your book.

a.	moon	crowd	root	school
b.	bedroom	bathroom	kitchen	dining room
c.	food	coconut	mood	brood
d.	goose	loose	fork	spoon
e.	school	soon	spoon	jungle
f.	seem	zoom	broom	room

2 Find words from the Word List that have a similar meaning to these words. Write the words in sentences in your book. The first one has been done for you.

a part of a house → *room* *I keep my room very tidy.*

a place to swim in →

you can see it in the sky at night →

the noise an owl makes →

the middle of the day →

not hot, but not very cold →

what you eat →

3 Write words from the Word List that fit into these word frames.

a. *m*

b. *g* 

c. *k* 

d. *b* 

e. *s* 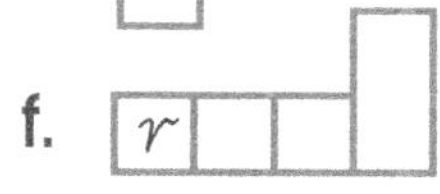

f. *r*

4 Change one letter in each word to make a new word. Write the new words in sentences in your book.

moon → *soon* → *I will leave soon.*

a. hoot → b. brood → c. loose → d. cool → e. mood →

! Challenge

- Join words together to make compound words that end with 'room', for example: *bed* + *room* = *bedroom*. How many words can you make?

5 Use the beginning and end sounds to write '**oo**' words.
Write the words in alphabetical order in your book. The first two have been done for you.

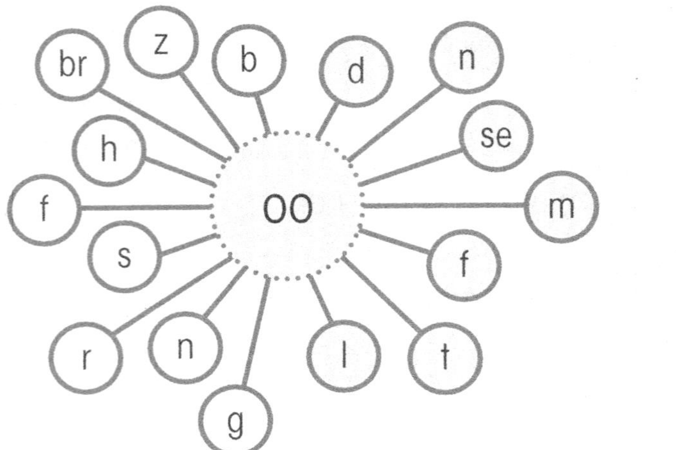

boot ____________ broom ____________

6 Choose words from the Word List to fill the gaps.
Write the complete sentences in your book.

a. The _ _ _ _ of the tree had grown under our house.
b. We used bamboo to make a _ _ _ _ for the hut.
c. There is a good swimming _ _ _ _ in our town.
d. The _ _ _ _ was very full last night.
e. The mudmen _ _ _ _ _ their prey with bows and arrows.

7 Find words from the Word List in this word search puzzle. Write them in your book.

c	b	o	o	t	r	o	o	f	x
p	c	b	a	l	l	o	o	n	s
n	k	g	o	o	s	e	t	o	o
b	c	a	z	o	o	m	i	d	n
b	e	d	r	o	o	m	t	p	j
m	f	o	o	d	p	c	o	o	l

8 Use this code to find words from the Word List. Write the words in your book.

CODE:

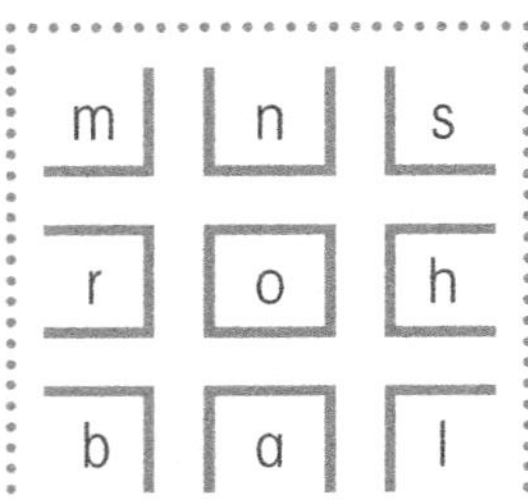

a.

b.

c.

d.

e.

WORD KNOWLEDGE > Conjunctions

RULE

A **conjunction** is a joining word, for example: *and, but, or, so, yet, because, as, if, both, before, since, like, for.* Maria went to the market <u>and</u> Pia went to the market. The preposition is 'and'.

1 Choose a conjunction from the Conjunction Box to complete these sentences. Write the complete sentences in your book.

a. Pia felt happy _ _ _ _ _ _ _ it was her birthday.
b. It was time to go _ _ I said goodbye.
c. We went to the market _ _ _ Jona came too.
d. We went shopping _ _ _ _ _ _ we went to the sing sing.
e. It was sad _ _ _ I didn't cry.

Conjunction BOX

so
but
because
and
before

2 Write sentences in your book with these conjunctions.

but because before so

COMMON WORDS >

1 Choose words from the Spelling List to fill the gaps. Write the complete sentences in your book.

a. I will post the _ _ _ _ _ _ to my aunt tomorrow.
b. Kali's little sister will _ _ _ in the 100-metre race.
c. Uncle Sam _ _ _ _ _ come to visit us tomorrow.
d. If you find the treasure, you might be allowed to _ _ _ _ it.
e. Do you think the horse will be able to _ _ _ _ over the fence?

Spelling LIST

jump
keep
letter
might
run
cool
tooth
spoon
roof
food

2 Write these words in sentences in your book. spoon roof cool

3 Write the words from the Spelling List in alphabetical order in your book.

Writing activity

- Imagine it is late at night. You and your friends are about to go on a midnight adventure. Write a story that begins like this: 'We got out of bed just before midnight because…'.

FOCUS > 'aw', 'ew', 'ow', 'oo' words

1 Write words in your book to keep the patterns going. The first one has been done for you.

a.	law	jaw	*draw*
b.	chew	threw	________
c.	drown	crown	________
d.	foot	hoot	________
e.	shower	power	________
f.	pawpaw	outlaw	________
g.	soon	boon	________

2 Choose the correct word. Write the complete sentences in your book.

a. The bright yellow (flower / shower) grew outside the window.
b. Simon was in a very bad (food / mood) today.
c. Pia thought she (new / knew) who her teacher was.
d. It is not good to eat (raw / paw) meat.
e. There was a big (crowd / crown) at the market today.
f. It is sometimes difficult to (stew / screw) the lid on the bottle.

3 Find the odd word out in each line. Write it in a sentence in your book.

a.	boot	toot	shoot	growl	root
b.	raw	draw	chew	saw	claw
c.	balloon	soon	eyebrow	goose	tooth
d.	growl	prowl	powder	shower	straw
e.	zoom	groom	boom	noon	clown

4 Write the complete words in your book.

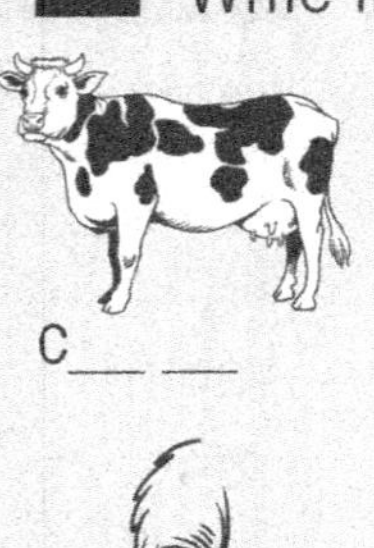
c_ _

s_ _ s_ _ _

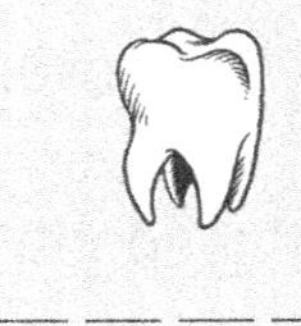
t_ _ _ _

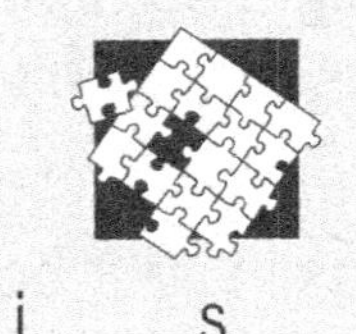
j_ _ s_ _

c_ _ _ _

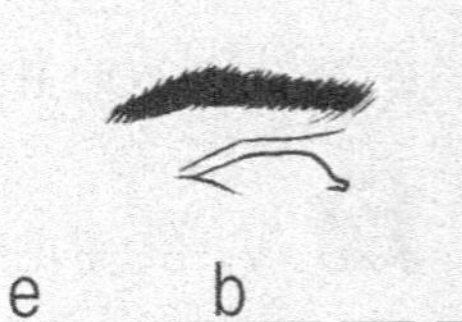
e_ _ b_ _ _

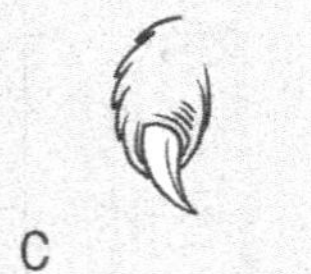
c_ _ _

c_ _ _ _

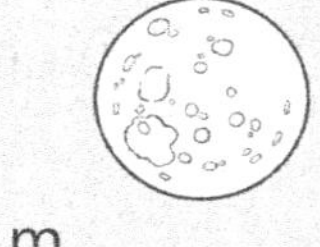
m_ _ _

j_ _ _ _

b_ _ r_ _ _

g_ _ _ _

s_ _ _ _ _

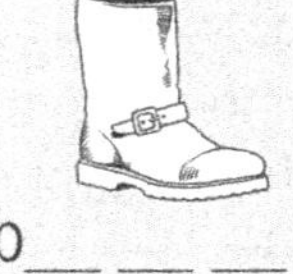
b_ _ _

g_ _ _ _

b_ _ _ _ _ _

5 Write as many words as you can in your book, using the magic word machines.

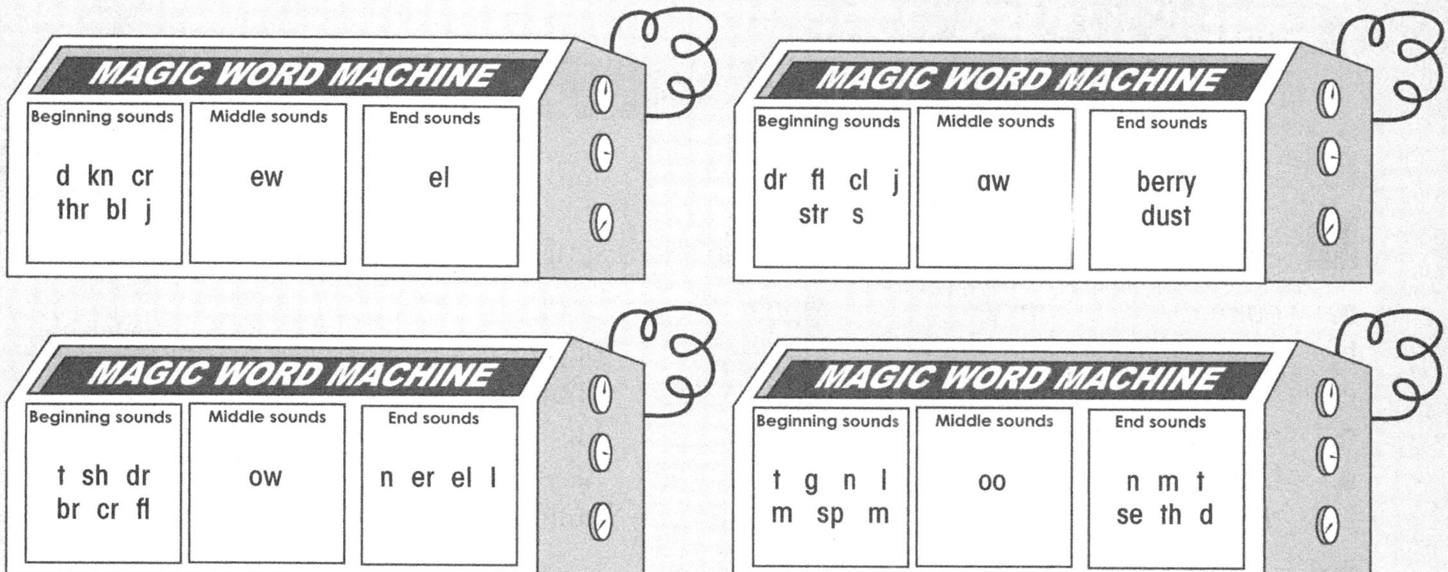

6 Change one letter in each word to make a new word that matches the clue. Write the new words in sentences in your book.

a. flaw (the hard, sharp nails on a bird's foot)
b. loose (a large kind of bird)
c. prowl (the noise an angry dog makes)
d. now (it gives us milk)
e. groom (you use it to sweep the floor)
f. drown (a king wears it on his head)
g. tower (you use it to dry yourself)
h. pew (something that is not old)

7 Sort these words into groups that have the same letters, for example: howl, prowl, growl. Write them in your book.

howl	prowl	growl	grew	roof
chew	tooth	claw	crown	boot
down	loose	brown	food	jewel
moon	balloon	zoom	power	paw

8 Build new words by adding '–s', '–ed' and '–ing' to these words. Write the new words in your book. The first one has been done for you.

a. cool → *cools cooled cooling*

b. claw **c.** prowl **d.** stew

FOCUS > 'air' words

Word LIST

hair
air
chair
fair
flair
stairs
fairy
dairy
airbag
aircraft
aircrew
airflow
airstrip
airport
airmail
chairlift
wheelchair
fairytale
hairdresser
pair
repair
hairy

1 Find the odd word out in each line. Write it in a sentence in your book.

a.	hair	dairy	repair	pool
b.	stairs	boil	fairy	airport
c.	pair	cloud	chair	chairlift
d.	airbag	straw	air	fair
e.	flower	flair	fair	fairytale
f.	aircraft	dairy	blew	hairdresser

2 Find words from the Word List that have a similar meaning to these words.
Write the words in sentences in your book.
The first one has been done for you.

a place where cows are milked → *dairy*
We went to the dairy to fetch some milk.

something you sit on → ______
lots of hair → ______
an air field → ______
two of a kind → ______
to fix something → ______
light in colour → ______
a small magic creature → ______
you breathe this → ______

3 Choose the correct word. Write the complete sentences in your book.

a. The plane landed on the (airstrip / church).
b. Uncle Sam sat on the (chair / television).
c. Kali went outside to get some fresh (air / trees).
d. The (clothesline / fairytale) that the teacher read was very scary.
e. I went to the hairdresser to get my (nails / hair) cut.
f. The (airbag / handbag) in the car saved the driver.
g. Mum bought a (pair / kilogram) of shoes for Jenifa.

Off the page

- Join words together to make compound words that start with 'air', for example: air + bag = airbag. How many words can you make?

4 Write words from the Word List that fit into these word frames.

a. c b. s c. w

d. h 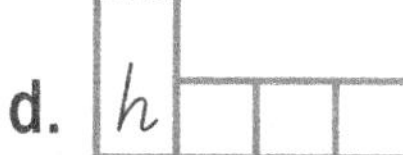 e. a f. h

5 Choose letters from the Letter Box to complete these words.
Write the words in sentences in your book.

__air __ __air __air__ __ __ __air

__air__ __ __air__ __ __air __air__

Letter BOX

d	ch
st	p
h	f
y	s
fl	rep

6 Choose words from the Word List to fill the gaps.
Write the complete sentences in your book.

a. The leg of the __ __ __ __ __ broke when the teacher sat on it.

b. Letti fell down the __ __ __ __ __ __ and hurt her head.

c. A great big __ __ __ __ __ gorilla swung on the branches.

d. I like the __ __ __ __ __ tale about Snow White.

e. We went to the __ __ __ __ __ farm to look at the cows.

f. "Open the window so we can get some fresh __ __ __."

7 Find words from the Word List in this word search puzzle. Write them in your book.

s	c	h	a	i	r	p	a	i
d	a	i	r	y	f	a	i	r
t	q	f	l	a	i	r	s	r
v	a	i	r	s	t	r	l	p
a	i	p	a	i	r	h	a	i
h	a	i	r	y	a	l	l	e

8 Use this code to find words from the Word List. Write the words in your book.

CODE:

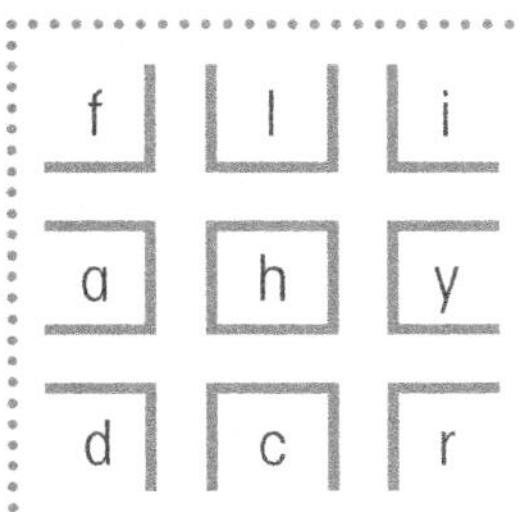

a. b.

c. d.

e. f.

WORD KNOWLEDGE > Antonyms

RULE

An **antonym** is a word that means the **opposite**.
For example: the antonym of *big* is *little* and the antonym of *hot* is *cold*.

1 Choose an antonym from the Antonym Box for these words.
Write each pair of words in your book.

a. night
b. in
c. boy
d. up
e. yes
f. hot

Antonym BOX

down
out
cold
day
no
girl

2 Find an antonym for the underlined word.
Write the new sentences in your book.

a. The <u>fast</u> runner came last in the race.
b. The duck dived into the <u>shallow</u> pond.
c. The garden was very <u>wet</u>.
d. It was so <u>hot</u> inside the room.
e. That is the <u>wrong</u> answer.

COMMON WORDS >

1 Choose words from the Spelling List to fill the gaps.
Write the complete sentences in your book.

a. I get up at eight _ _ _ _ _ _ _ every morning.
b. If you add five eggs to two eggs, you get _ _ _ _ _ eggs.
c. Ben likes to _ _ _ _ his bike to the market.
d. Yesterday Joni wore the _ _ _ _ clothes again.
e. Pia received a silver medal for coming _ _ _ _ _ _ in the race.

Spelling LIST

o'clock
ride
same
second
seven
chair
pair
air
hair
stairs

2 Write these words in sentences in your book.

stairs pair air

3 Write the words from the Spelling List in alphabetical order in your book.

Writing activity

- Write about three things you don't want to do tomorrow.
  Explain why you don't want to do these things.

FOCUS > 'ar' words

Word LIST

car
bar
jar
bark
arm
carport
carpet
barn
dark
harm
farm
farmyard
art
far
mark
star
start
starlight
shark
smart
tart
mark
park
March
part
party

1 Find the odd word out in each line. Write it in a sentence in your book.

a.	car	arm	chair	jar
b.	carport	airport	farm	carpet
c.	mark	park	pork	bark
d.	airbag	dark	March	carport
e.	sunlight	starlight	car	park
f.	arm	firm	farm	army

2 Find words from the Word List that have a similar meaning to these words. Write the words in sentences in your book. The first one has been done for you.

the noise a dog makes → *bark* *That dog has a loud bark.*

this twinkles in the sky → ______ not light → ______

a large fish with sharp teeth → ______ you drive this on the road → ______

a soft covering for the floor → ______ the third month of the year → ______

a container made of glass → ______

3 Write words from the Word List that fit into these word frames.

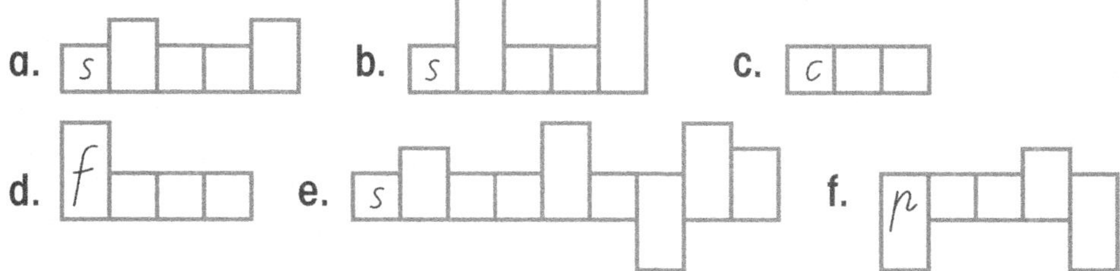

4 Choose the correct word. Write the complete sentences in your book.

a. We can (smart / park) the car near the tree.
b. Tandi broke her (harm / arm) when she fell over.
c. My dad is going to (start / part) building a new house.
d. We are all going to the (jar / park) to have a picnic.
e. Mum is making a cake for Michael's birthday (star / party).
f. The big white (arm / shark) came close to the swimmers.

5 Use the beginning and end sounds to write '**ar**' words.
Write the words in alphabetical order in your book.
The first two have been done for you.

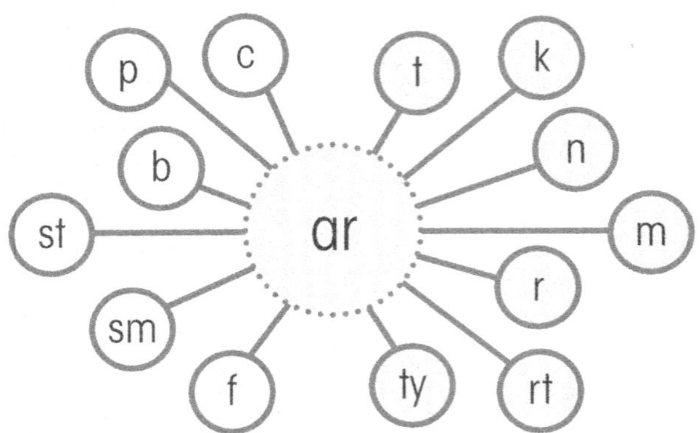

party	*smart*

6 Choose words from the Word List to fill the gaps.
Write the complete sentences in your book.

a. Dad put the car in the _ _ _ _ _ _ _.
b. When the moon went behind the clouds, the sky became _ _ _ _.
c. All the farm animals were locked in the _ _ _ _.
d. Lelti had a black _ _ _ _ on her arm.
e. The jam _ _ _ broke when Maria dropped it.
f. All the runners were ready for the _ _ _ _ _ of the race.
g. Mum said to take the baby to the _ _ _ _ for a game.

7 Use this code to find words from the Word List. Write the words in your book.

CODE:

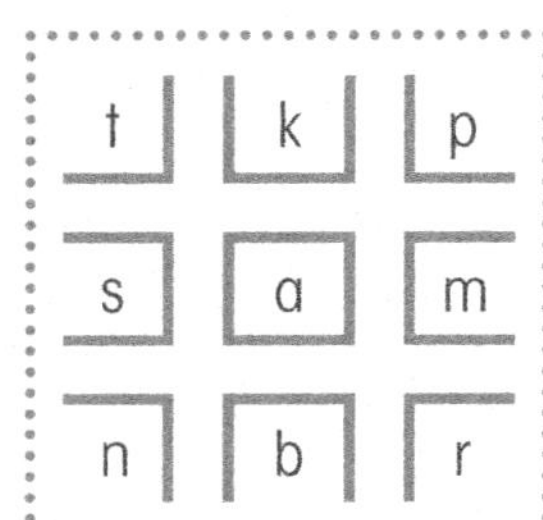

a.
b.
c.
d.
e.
f.
g.
h.
i.
j.
k.
l.

WORD KNOWLEDGE > Synonyms

RULE

An **synonym** is a word that means the **same**, for example: a synonym for *big* is *large*, a synonym for *small* is *little* and a synonym for *sob* is *cry*.

1 Choose two or more synonyms from the Synonym Box for these words. Write each group of words in your book.

a. good **b.** small **c.** bad **d.** yelled

2 Use the picture clues to find synonyms from the Word Bank for these words. The first one has been done for you.

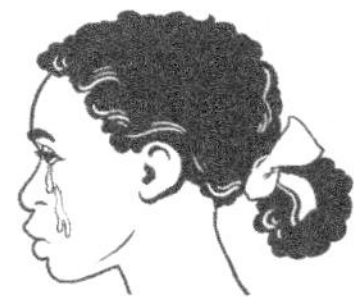

thin, skinny

Word BANK

cup thin sob run sprint skinny cool ocean cold cry sea mug

Synonym BOX

excellent
crayon
great
huge
table
little
tiny
clever
rotten
car
excited
naughty
very
shouted
screamed
lovely

COMMON WORDS >

1 Choose words from the Spelling List to fill the gaps. Write the complete sentences in your book.

a. You must __ __ __ __ __ __ look both ways before you cross the road.

b. A tiger has __ __ __ __ __ __ and black stripes.

c. Nina said, "I __ __ __ __ __ I can spell this word."

d. Simon decided to __ __ __ __ home from school today.

e. I'm going to the market to __ __ __ a new shirt.

2 Write these words in sentences in your book.

party harm smart

3 Write the words from the Spelling List in alphabetical order in your book.

Writing activity

- Would you like to have a twin sister or brother? Write some good and bad things about being a twin.

Spelling LIST

think
walk
yellow
always
buy
smart
mark
party
harm
dark

Unit 38

FOCUS > 'or' words

Word LIST

for
horn
corn
born
torn
worn
form
sort
short
sport
morning
thunderstorm
corner
torch
north
horse
force
popcorn
forget
storm
fort

1 Find the odd word out in each line. Write it in a sentence in your book.

a.	sort	dark	fort	storm
b.	horn	born	barn	torn
c.	corner	force	form	sharp
d.	forget	popcorn	ice cream	horse
e.	south	north	torch	worn
f.	sort	short	smell	sport

2 Find words from the Word List that have a similar meaning to these words. Write the words in sentences in your book. The first one has been done for you.

to not remember → *forget I forget where I have to go.*

not tall → __________

the opposite of south → __________

the part of a car that beeps → __________

ripped apart → __________

wild wind and rain → __________

3 Write words from the Word List that fit into these word frames.

a. 
h

b. t

c. c

d. s

e. c

f. t

g. 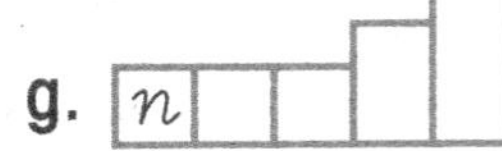
n

h. 
p

i. 
s

RHYME time > Copy this rhyme into your book and then ...

1. Underline all the '**or**' words.
2. Write five words that rhyme with 'horn'.

Little Boy Blue
Come blow your horn
There are cows to be milked
And sheep to be shorn.

Come back Boy Blue!
Come blow your horn!
Come back to your sheep
And your cows in the corn.

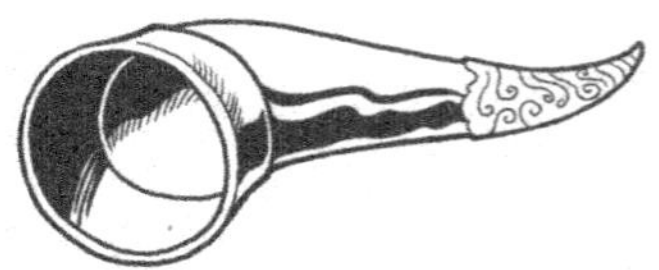

4 Choose the correct word. Write the complete sentences in your book.

a. The baby was (born / short) on the first day of the month.
b. Grandma took the dog (form / for) a walk.
c. Letti rode the (horse / sport) to the market.
d. Simon joined the police (storm / force) when he was eighteen.
e. The shirt was so old that it had (worn / storm) out.
f. When we turned around the (horn / corner) we saw our friend.

5 Write as many words as you can in your book, using the magic word machine.

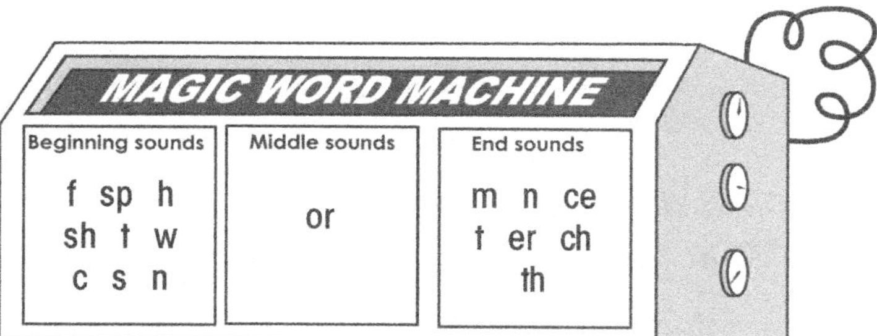

6 Choose words from the Word List to fill the gaps.
Write the complete sentences in your book.

a. We have to get up early in the _ _ _ _ _ _ _ to catch the bus.
b. There was fierce lightning when the _ _ _ _ _ hit the town.
c. If we run fast we will get there in a _ _ _ _ _ time.
d. When the lights went out I used the _ _ _ _ _ to see.
e. My favourite _ _ _ _ _ is puk puk rugby.
f. Lani is too _ _ _ _ _ to reach the top shelf.
g. Mrs Bula Bula has _ _ _ _ her special necklace today.

7 Use this code to find words from the Word List. Write the words in your book.

CODE:

a.
b.
c.
d.
e.
f.
g.
h.
i.

WORD KNOWLEDGE > Prefixes

RULE

A **prefix** is added to the front of a word to change its meaning, for example: *un* + *kind* = *unkind*.
When '**un–**' is added to 'kind' it changes the word to the opposite meaning.

1 Add the prefix '**un–**' to these words to make words with the opposite meaning.
Write three of the words in sentences in your book.

a. even **b.** happy **c.** pack **d.** wise **e.** safe **f.** able

2 Write this pair of words in a sentence of your own.

fold / unfold

3 Add the prefix '**dis–**' to these words to make words with the opposite meaning.
Write three of the words in sentences in your book.

a. like **b.** appear **c.** agree **d.** infect **e.** obey **f.** place

COMMON WORDS >

1 Choose words from the Spelling List to fill the gaps.
Write the complete sentences in your book.

a. When you add four to four you get _ _ _ _ _.

b. You must have _ _ _ _ _ hands before you eat.

c. Uncle Sam _ _ _ _ fishing every morning.

d. The _ _ _ _ of our house is made from wood.

e. When you climb the tree for coconuts be careful not to _ _ _ _.

Spelling LIST

clean
door
eight
fall
goes
born
storm
corner
north
force

2 Write these words in sentences in your book.

north storm corner

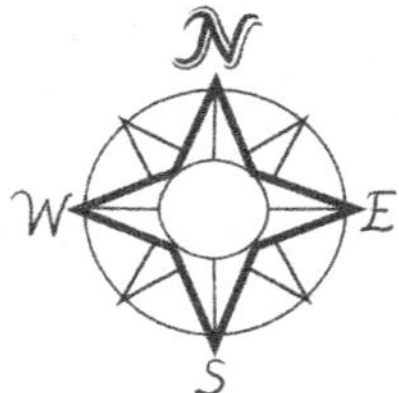

3 Write the words from the Spelling List in alphabetical order in your book.

Writing activity

- What is your favourite sport?
Write about what the sport is, how you play it and why you like it.

FOCUS > 'oo' words (as in 'book')

Word LIST

book
look
took
cook
hook
brook
crook
shook
soot
wood
good
hood
stood
wool
firewood
cookbook

1 Find the odd word out in each line. Write it in a sentence in your book.

a.	wool	book	show	hood
b.	crowd	stood	wood	book
c.	look	hook	crawl	shook
d.	brook	enjoy	crook	took
e.	firewood	cookbook	boil	good
f.	soot	today	look	brook

2 Find words from the Word List that have a similar meaning to these words. Write the words in sentences in your book. The first one has been done for you.

a small stream or creek → *brook*

The bubbling brook sparkled in the sunlight.

a head cover that is joined to your jumper →

to heat or prepare food →

you use this to catch fish →

you read this →

this comes from a tree →

this grows on a sheep →

this contains recipes →

3 Write words from the Word List that fit into these word frames.

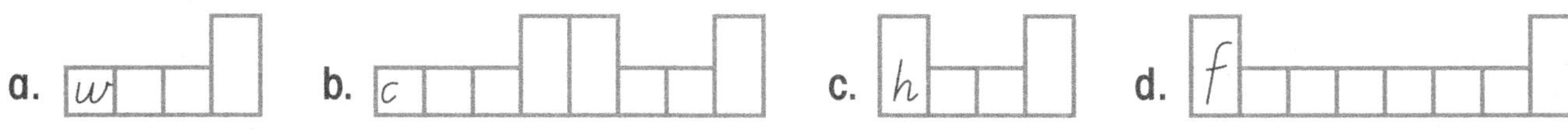

! Challenge

- Join two words together to make compound words that begin or end with 'wood'. For example: *ply + wood = plywood, wood + pile = woodpile.* How many words can you make that begin or end with 'wood'?

- Choose one word beginning with 'wood' and one word ending with 'wood'. Write them in sentences in your book.

4 Change one letter in each word to make a new word.
Write the new words in sentences in your book. The first one has been done for you.

hood → *good* → *I will be good today at school.*

a. book → **b.** crook → **c.** good → **d.** wool → **e.** hook →

5 Write as many words as you can in your book, using the magic word machine.

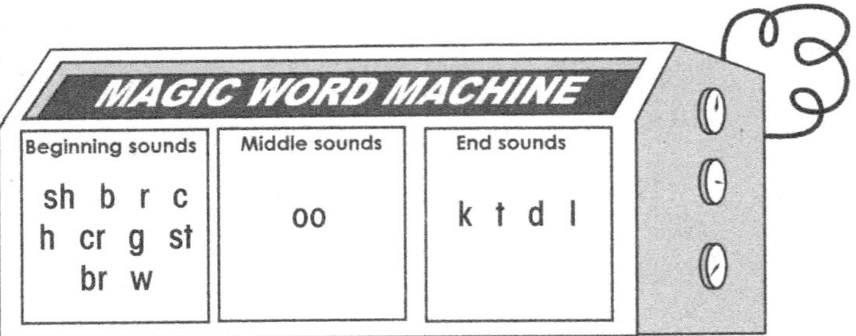

6 Choose words from the Word List to fill the gaps.
Write the complete sentences in your book.

a. If you are very _ _ _ _, we will go to the sing sing tonight.
b. Look at all the black _ _ _ _ in the chimney.
c. I will need a really big _ _ _ _ to catch that fish.
d. The dog _ _ _ _ _ its body and a flea jumped out of its fur.
e. It's my turn to _ _ _ _ the lunch today.
f. Mrs Pena read us a _ _ _ _ in the library.
g. Kali was in trouble because he _ _ _ _ Simon's book.

7 Find words from the Word List in this word search puzzle. Write them in your book.

z	v	c	o	o	k	l	o	o
g	g	o	o	d	b	o	o	k
j	f	i	r	e	w	o	o	d
c	r	o	o	k	s	h	o	o
a	a	a	b	b	o	o	k	a
j	s	t	o	o	k	l	m	l

WORD KNOWLEDGE > Suffixes

RULE

A **suffix** is added to the end of a word, for example: *jump + ed = jumped, jump + ing = jumping.*

1 Add the suffix '**–ed**' to these words. Write the words in your book.
Write three of the words in sentences in your book.

a. look b. climb c. play d. push e. kick f. work

2 Add the suffix '**–ing**' to these words. Write the words in your book.
Write three of the words in sentences in your book.

a. eat b. blow c. cry d. kneel e. shout f. lick

COMMON WORDS >

1 Choose words from the Spelling List to fill the gaps.
Write the complete sentences in your book.

a. If you listen carefully, you can _ _ _ _ the clock tick.
b. Peta has much _ _ _ _ _ _ legs than Meri.
c. If you come _ _ _ _ _ in the race you will get a bronze medal.
d. The horse bucked and Mrs Pena fell _ _ _.
e. Lani had to _ _ _ _ her picture to the teacher.

Weekly Spelling list to be tested at the end of the week.

2 Write these words in sentences in your book.

book good wool

Spelling LIST

hear
longer
off
show
third
book
good
stood
wool
shook

3 Write the words from the Spelling List in alphabetical order in your book.

Writing activity

- Make your own book. Make a cover and write a title.
  Write a story inside and draw some pictures.
  Staple the pages to the cover and then read your book to a friend.

Revision

Focus: 'air', 'ar', 'or', 'oo' words

1 Write words in your book to keep the patterns going.

a.	chair	pair	hair	e.	corner	storm	________
b.	farm	farmer	________	f.	stair	repair	________
c.	horn	born	________	g.	stood	cookbook	________
d.	book	hook	________				

2 Choose the correct word. Write the complete sentences in your book.

a. We drove the car into the (carpet / carport).
b. We are playing (sport / horse) this afternoon.
c. The shearer collected all the (wool / wood) from the sheep.
d. The pilot landed the plane on the (wheelchair / airstrip).
e. Uncle Sam has very (dairy / hairy) arms.
f. The (car / shark) took a big bite out of his leg.
g. Dad said that Pia was a very (good / crook) girl.
h. Aunty Lina's (hair / chair) went curly when she washed it.

3 Find the odd word out in each line. Write it in a sentence in your book.

a.	hood	good	wood	stood	crowd
b.	aircraft	airmail	farmyard	airport	air
c.	starlight	moonlight	mark	park	carpark
d.	north	storm	south	force	ford
e.	fairy	dairy	airy	air	wind

4 Write the complete words in your book.

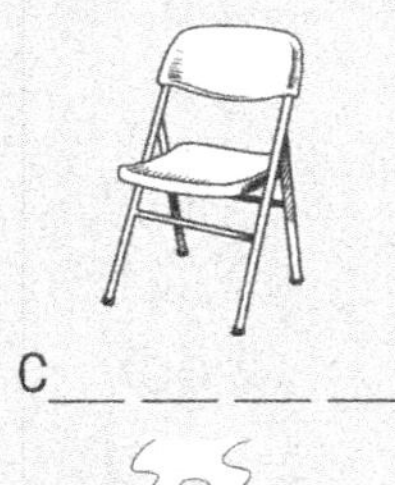
c__ __ __ __

b__ __ __

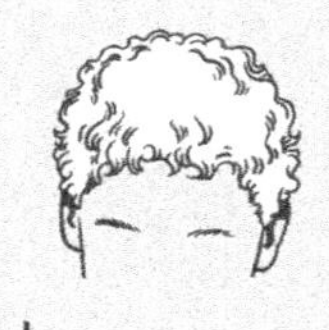
h__ __ __

f__ __ __ __

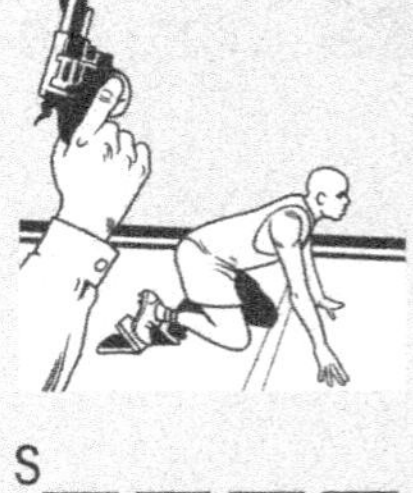
s__ __ __ __

c__ __ __

h__ __ __ __

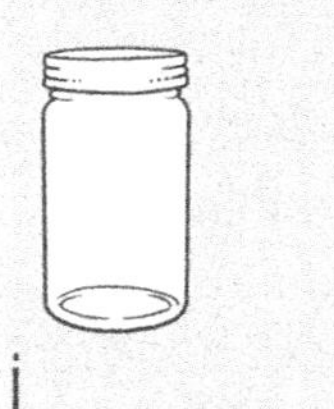
j__ __

s__ __ __ __

s__ __ __ __

5 Write as many words as you can in your book, using the magic word machines.

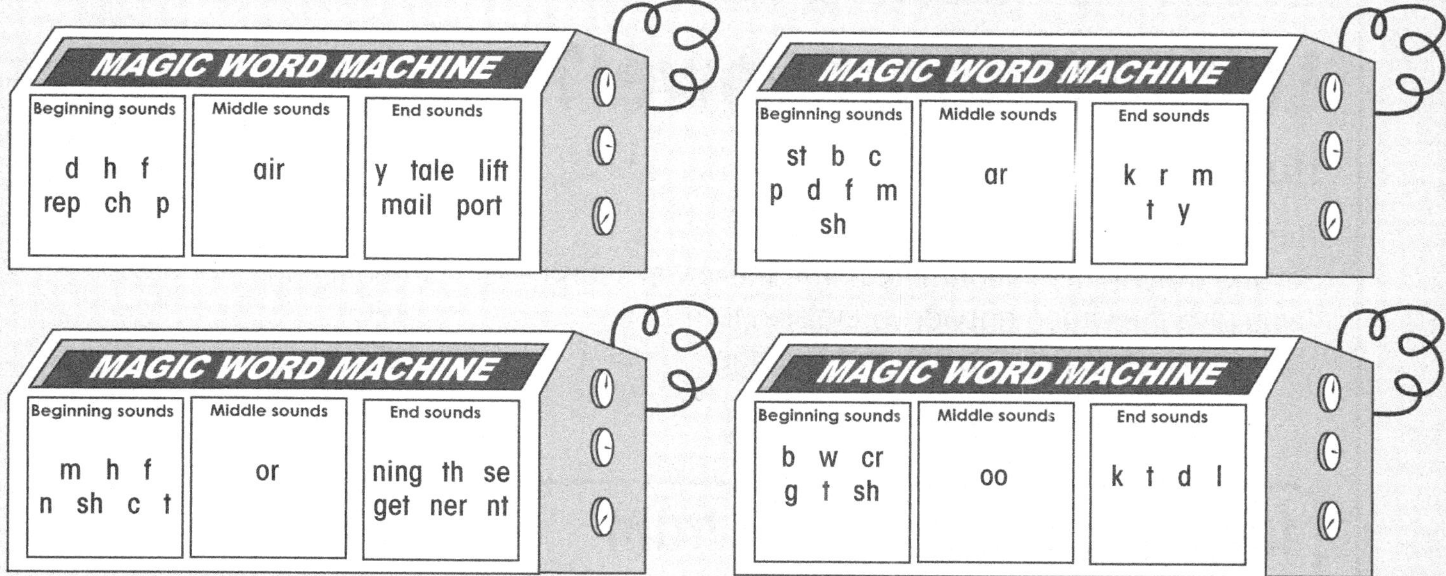

6 Change one letter in each word to make a new word that matches the clue. Write the new words in sentences in your book.

a. horn (a time when some one first came into the world)
b. took (you do this to make a meal)
c. sport (not very tall)
d. dairy (a magical creature with wings)
e. porch (you use this to shine a light in the dark)
f. mark (not light)
g. cord (you cook this to make popcorn)
h. smart (to begin or set off)

7 Sort these words into groups that have the same letters, for example: art, arm, party. Write them in your book.

hook	art	harm	torch	force	hair
cook	chair	arm	shook	party	wood
starlight	horse	repair	wool	morning	carport
dairy	sport	book	fair	popcorn	

8 Build new words by adding '–s', '–ed' and '–ing' to these base words. Write the new words in your book. The first one is done for you.

a. look → *looks looked looking*

b. cook c. park d. mark e. pair
f. air g. corner h. sort

Long or short vowel?

START

How to play

Throw a dice to move a step.
Say the word in the square and name the vowel sound – is it long or short?
If you give the wrong answer you miss a turn.
The first player to reach home is the winner.

face

home

train

goat

pig

blue

sing

swim

play

smile

wheat

knife

jump

read

ten

cake

pet 

hat 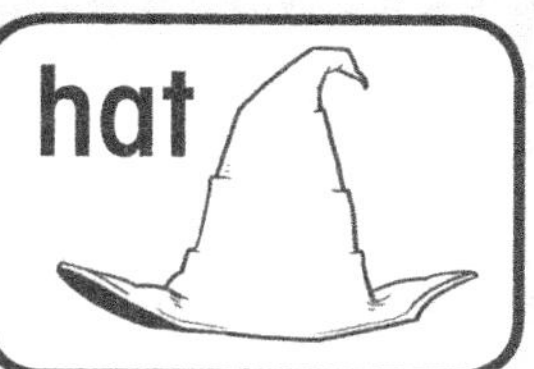

kiss 

sand 

gate 

sun 

rose 

plane 

line 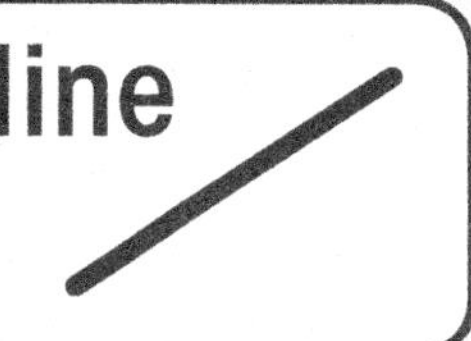

sock 

match 

run 

plate 

FINISH

cat 

chicken 

cute 

sea 

cod 

Get to the top of the mountain!

How to play

Throw a dice to move a step.
Say a word that rhymes with the word you land on.
If you can't say a word, you miss a turn.
The first player to reach the top of the mountain is the winner.

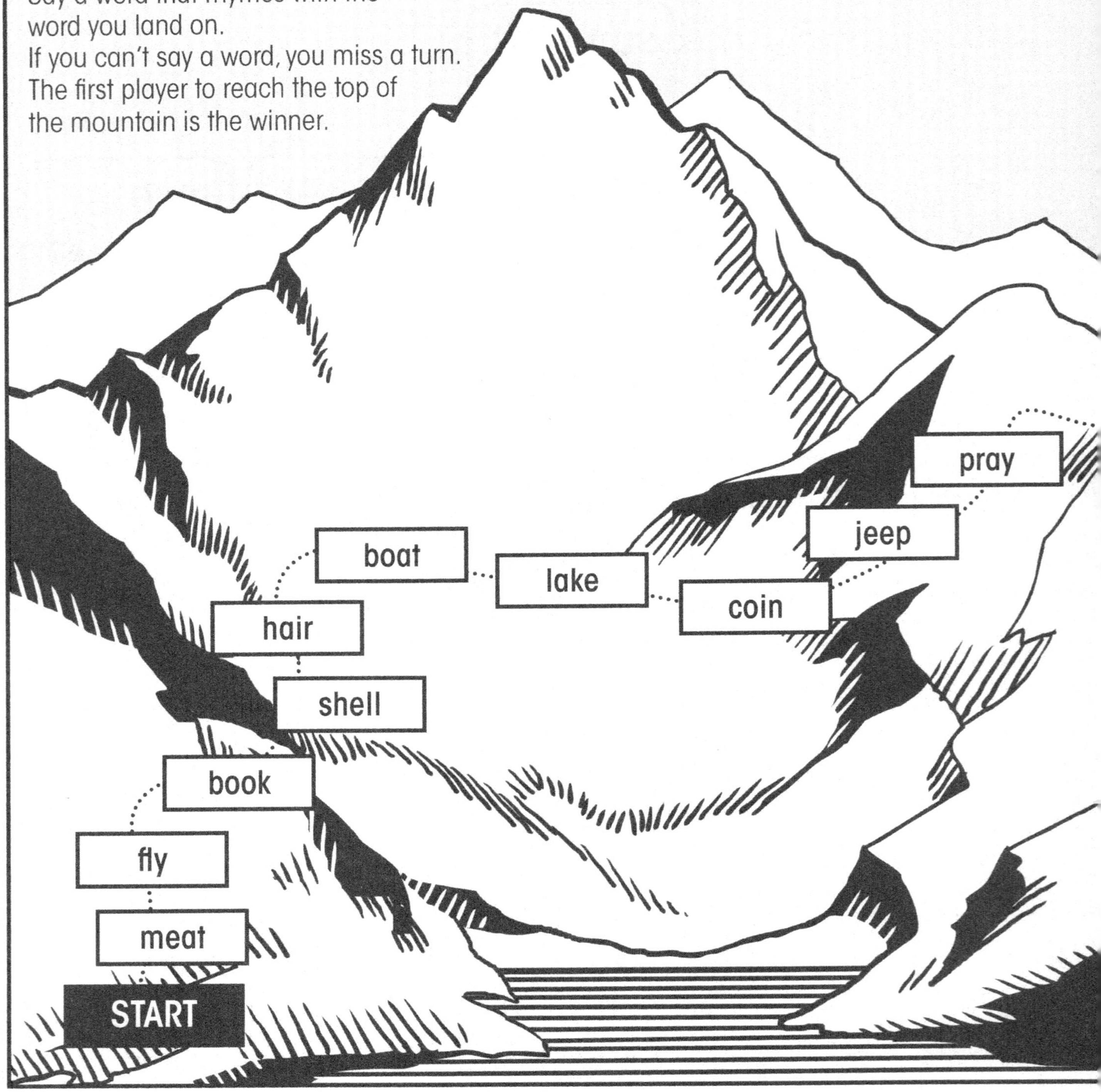

START
meat
fly
book
shell
hair
boat
lake
coin
jeep
pray

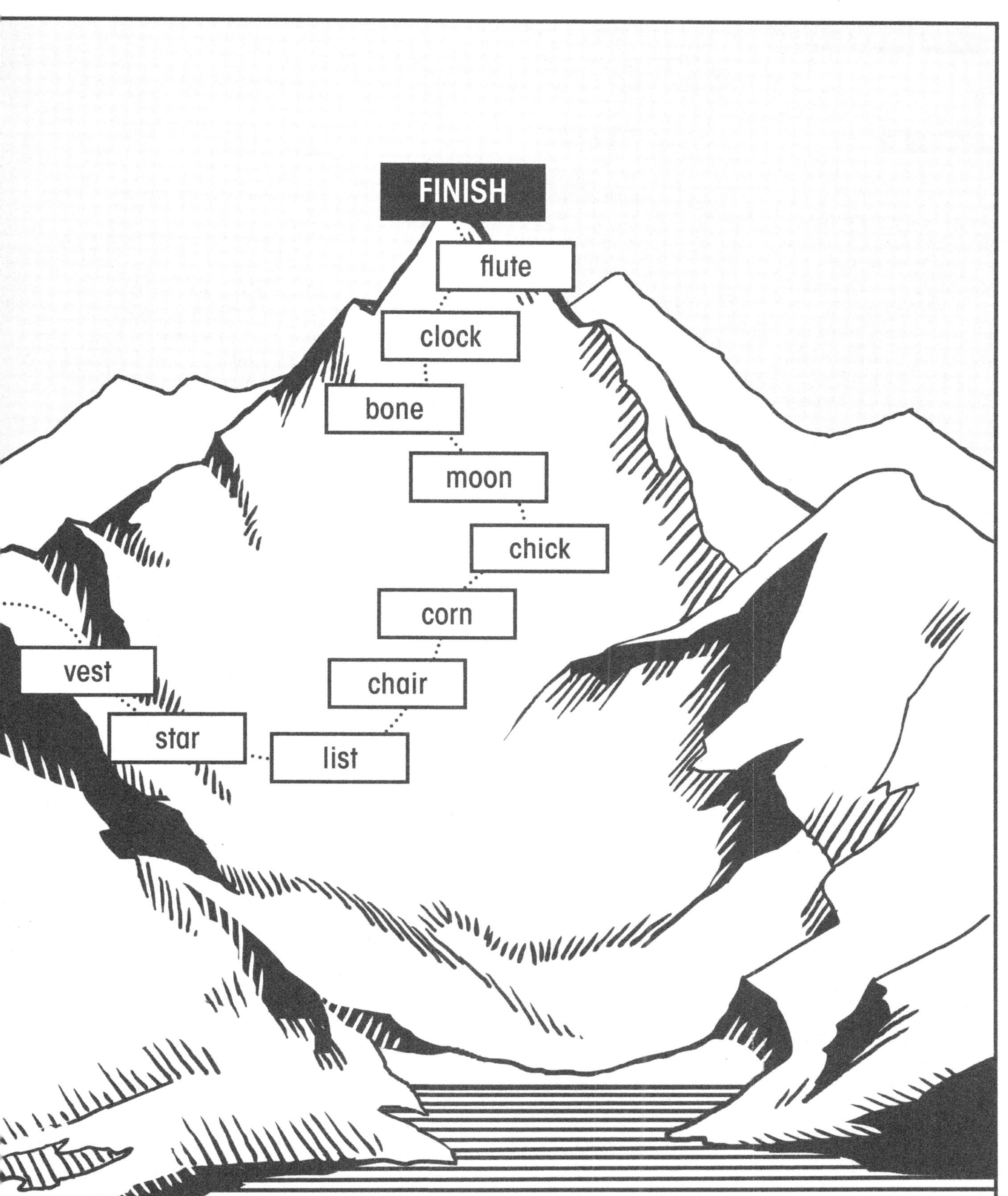
FINISH
flute
clock
bone
moon
chick
corn
chair
list
star
vest

Answers

Unit 1

3 brush, dish, fish, shark, shell, shirt, shoe
4 **a** fish; **b** sharp; **c** ship; **d** wash; **e** flash
5 Many answers, for example: ship, shape, flash, brush, etc.
6 shout, dish, cash, dash, shut
7 **a** Possible answers: cash, dash, lash, mash, rash
b Possible answers: fish, swish
c Possible answers: gush, hush, lush
8 **a** shut; **b** brush; **c** shell; **d** shirt; **e** shoe

WORD KNOWLEDGE >

1 sheets, shops, sharks, ships
2 shirts, shells, shoes, sheds, shins, shovels

COMMON WORDS >

1 are; **2** your; **3** was; **4** were; **5** you

Unit 2

1 chill, chop, chunk, child, chip, chick; lunch, teach, torch, beach, pinch, bunch
3 beach, branch, cheek, chin, chip, chop, pinch, touch
4 **a** beach; **b** chair; **c** chop; **d** cheek; **e** branch
5 **a** Possible answers: beach, peach
b Possible answers: bunch, lunch, munch
6 Many answers, for example: chip, chat, chick, choke, beach, torch, punch, etc.
7 chop, chick, torch, child, beach

WORD KNOWLEDGE >

1 combs, dishes, chickens, beaches, rocks, matches, torches, chains, cheeks, churches, punches, brushes, shirts, sashes, ships, peaches
2 box, punch, lunch, ash
3 torches, branches, wishes, fish

COMMON WORDS >

1 **a** have; **b** child; **c** said; **d** many; **e** bunch

Unit 3

1 thorn, this, thug, thick, think, they; teeth, path, truth, month, both, tenth
3 bath, month, north, teeth, thick, thin, thorn, tooth
4 **a** them; **b** truth; **c** month; **d** thick; **e** thorn
5 third, fifth, sixth, seventh, tenth
6 Many answers, for example: thin, think, bath, tooth
7 thick, mouth, bath, path, thorn
8 their, them, then, there, these, they

COMMON WORDS >

1 **a** there; **b** their
3 **a** third; **b** would; **c** some; **d** more; **e** write

Unit 4

1 whale, whip, why, where, white, when, what, which
3 whale, wheat, whip, whirlwind, whiskers, whistle
4 **a** white; **b** why; **c** when; **d** where; **e** whip; **f** wheat; **g** which; **h** white
5 whisk, why, whiz, what
6 Many answers, for example: when, white, whole
7 wheelbarrow, white, whip, wheat, whiskers, wheels

WORD KNOWLEDGE >

1 house, fireman, pot, lion

COMMON WORDS >

1 **a** water; **b** because; **c** people; **d** could; **e** come

Unit 5 REVISION

FOCUS > 'sh' and 'ch' words

1 ship, shop, shelf, shark, sheep, shirt, shout;
fish, dish, wish, cash, dash, mash, flash, sash, brush, ash, crush, hush, mush;
chop, chip, chap, chick, chair, chain, chin, check, chill;
teach, peach, each, torch, beach, punch, branch, lunch, bench, hunch, brunch
2 Possible answers:
dish, swish; sash, rash; beach, teach; punch, bunch
3 fish, sheep, chain, shark, torch, chair, ship, punch

FOCUS > 'th' and 'wh–' words

1 thin, thick, thug, third, thorn, then, third, the; bath, both, tooth, north, south, month, fifth, path, sixth, tenth; wheat, why, which, whale, whisker, where, whisper, what, wheel, whizz, wheelbarrow, whistle
2 whiskers, tooth, thorn, wheel, whisper, teeth, path, wheat
3 **a** thick; **b** where; **c** month; **d** wheel; **e** what; **f** tooth

Unit 6

1 chest, twist, stop, star, stem, storm, frost, first
3 **a** vest; **b** wrist; **c** gust; **d** stem; **e** study; **f** west; **g** rest; **h** star; **i** stand
4 **a** nest; **b** crust; **c** cost; **d** fist; **e** study; **f** west
5 cost, star, fist, rest, stop, test
6 wrist, nest, stop, mist, crust, test
7 stand, stem, star, step, stop, study
8 twist, gust, chest, pest, trust, wrist

WORD KNOWLEDGE >

1 We had fun at the sing sing. Mum and Dad came with their friends Joe and Kila. We all dressed up in beads and feathers. Some of the dancers had masks. My sister played the kundu drum. We went home late. It was a lot of fun.

COMMON WORDS >

1 asked; **2** after; **3** storm; **4** here; **5** how

Unit 7

1 pack, neck, sick, sock, luck, black, check, stick, clock, stuck
3 **a** track; **b** wreck; **c** struck; **d** brick; **e** frock; **f** duck; **g** stack; **h** shock

4 **a** black; **b** neck; **c** truck; **d** sick; **e** shock
5 tick, flock, speck, truck, peck, shack
6 **a** snack; **b** chuck; **c** crack; **d** block; **e** quick; **f** rack;

WORD KNOWLEDGE >

1 **a** Her mother came outside.
b The mouse was quick, but the cat was quicker.
c I saw the track in the bush.
d There was a speck of milk on the tablecloth.

COMMON WORDS >

1 look; **2** mother; **3** our; **4** them; **5** that

Unit 8

1 catch, sketch, switch, clutch, crutch, match, pitch
3 **a** pitch; **b** catch; **c** latch; **d** scratch; **e** hutch; **f** hatch
4 **a** back; **b** rich; **c** which; **d** hutch
5 hutch, hatch, catch, thatch, fetch, patch
6 **a** patch; **b** notch; **c** retch; **d** clutch; **e** ditch; **f** latch

WORD KNOWLEDGE >

1 **a** growled; **b** jumped; **c** mooed; **d** purred; **e** climbed; **f** galloped

COMMON WORDS >

1 they; **2** then; **3** this; **4** when; **5** where

Unit 9

1 bubble, rabbit, scribble;
ladder, daddy, middle, puddle, cuddle;
biggest, juggle, giggle;
carry, sorry, hurry, sorrow;
fizz, buzz, puzzle, dazzle
3 juggle, ladder, puddle, bubble, carrot, puzzle, egg, rabbit
4 **a** cubby; **b** puzzle; **c** rubbish **d** wriggle; **e** wagging; **f** hurry; **g** hidden
5 riddle, buzz, fizzy, giggle, egg, dazzle, ladder, daddy, wagging, carrot, rubbish, hidden, curry, middle, sorry, biggest, hurry, carry, sizzle, puddle
6 rubbish, daddy, puzzle, carrot, curry
7 **a** hurry; **b** carry; **c** wiggle; **d** riddle; **e** ladder; **f** sizzle
8 **a** sorry; **b** riddle; **c** ladder; **d** sizzle; **e** egg

COMMON WORDS >

1 down; **2** know; **3** first; **4** who; **5** than

Unit 10 REVISION

1 star, still, step, stand, stick, storm;
nest, rest, test, cost, fist, just;
lock, lick, clock, flock, neck, sock,
back, clock, truck, stick;
crutch, catch, match, fetch,
blotch, patch
2 Possible answers:
nest, test; tack, stack; must, trust;
lick, quick; list, fist; match, hatch
3 **a** lock; **b** cost; **c** patch; **d** match; **e** test; **f** flock
4 neck, clock, brick, patch, witch, fist, pest, quack, scratch, sock, match, truck
5 **b** dust; **c** rest; **d** nest; **e** clock; **f** sick; **g** peck; **h** stick; **i** lost; **j** witch; **k** duck
6 list, tick, dust, speck, such, luck
7 **a** Possible answers:
start, storm, stock, stick
b Possible answers:
batch, fetch, ditch, catch
c Possible answers:
clock, stock, shock, block
d Possible answers:
whack, black, slack, shack
e Possible answers:
nest, best, pest, list

Unit 11

1 made, cane, cape, pane, hate, pale, plane, mate, shame
2 scrap, fad, rat
3 **a** spade; **b** male; ram; **c** hat; **d** face; **e** gale; **f** stag; **g** rate
4 Possible answers:
trace, lace, mace; hate, fate, late;
bake, cake, lake; male, bale, gale;
tame, frame, shame
5 face, spade, gale, whale, plane, male, gate, fake
6 Many answers; for example:
take, skate, shade, wage, etc.
7 **a** shade/spade/stage/scale/stale/shape/shave, crane/crate
b face/fade/fake/fame, place/blade/blame/flame/plane
c shade/whale/shape/shave, bake/cake/fake/lake
d came/fame/game, grace/place/blade/grade/shade/spade/stage/brake/scale/whale/blame/flame/frame/ crane/plane/grape/shape/crate/shave

WORD KNOWLEDGE >

Last week Mum, my sister Sal and I went to the market in Port Moresby. We bought a bilum for my sister and a table for Grandpa Joe.

In the afternoon we had lunch with our friend Lia. She bought some food for her pet dog Tibbles and her pet cat Dribbles.

It was late before we went home and we were very tired when at last we arrived at our village. It was a good day. We all enjoyed our time at Port Moresby.

COMMON WORDS >

1 **a** back; **b** call; **c** each

Unit 12

1 pine, site, kite, dime, spice, hide, crime, grime, slime
2 strip, quit, bite, win, rid
3 **a** wise; **b** prize; **c** wide; **d** white; **e** ripe; **f** spine
4 Possible answers:
line, shine, nine; mite, bite, site;
pipe, tripe, wipe; nice, dice, lice;
tide, side, wide; hike, pike, spike
5 twine, sprite, spice, bride, wife, wine, nine
6 Many answers; for example:
nine, stride, white, splice, etc.
7 **a** spice/spike/spine, price/spice/bride/glide/guide/pride/slide/spike/smile/stile/prize/crime/grime/slime/spine/swine/twine/quite/white/gripe
b dice/dime/dine, price/spice/bride/glide/guide/pride/slide/spike/smile/stile/prize/crime/grime/slime/spine/swine/twine/quite/white/gripe
c spike, dice/lice/mice/nice/rice/hide/ride/side/wide/bike/hike/like/pike/file/mile/pile/rise/wise/size/life/wife/dime/dine/nine/pine/wine/bite/site/ripe/pipe
d spice/slide/spike/smile/stile/slime/spine/swine, dice/lice/mice/nice/rice/hide/ride/side/wide/bike/hike/like/pike/file/mile/pile/rise/wise/size/life/wife/dime/dine/nine/pine/wine/bite/site/ripe/pipe

WORD KNOWLEDGE >

1 a Tai lives in Bougainville.
  b My sister went to Lae.
  c Port Moresby is the capital of Papua New Guinea.
  d The river Fly flows past our village.
  e A high mountain in Papua New Guinea is Albert Edward.

COMMON WORDS >

1 kind; **2** girl; **3** ear; **4** home; **5** far

Unit 13

1 mope, hope, tone, lope, pope, slope, scope, zone, cope
2 ton, hop, slop, pop
3 **a** broke; **b** nose; **c** slope; **d** rope; **e** hose; **f** gnome, home; **g** awoke, smoke
4 Possible answers: woke, stroke, choke; hose, pose, nose; bone, cone, stone; mope, hope, rope; home, tome
5 joke, home, stone, spoke, broke, froze, throne, rose
6 Many answers; for example: nose, slope, gnome, those, etc.
7 a smoke/spoke/stone/scope/slope
  b cone/cope, bloke/broke/choke/smoke/spoke/awoke/gnome/prose/those/chose/froze/clone/drone/phone/prone/stone/grope/scope/slope/elope
  c spoke, joke/poke/woke/dome/home/hose/pose/rose/doze/bone/cone/lone/tone/zone/cope/hope/lope/mope/pope/rope
  d smoke/spoke/stone/scope/slope, nose

COMMON WORDS >

1 **a** people; **b** only; **c** last; **d** name; **e** made
3 choke, home, last, made, name, only, people, phone, rope, smoke

Unit 14

1 fuse, cute, rude, flute, lute, amuse, exclude, rule, June
2 cut, us
3 **a** pollute; **b** cute; **c** juice; **d** use; **e** rude; **f** use; **g** salute
4 Possible answers: rude, nude; cute, flute; use, fuse; tune, rune
5 nude, excuse, June, prune, confused, rude, flute, dune
6 Many answers; for example: rude, mute, fuse, etc.
7 a crude/chute, mute/muse
  b rude/ruse/rule, crude/brute/chute/flute/amuse/abuse/prune
  c brute, fuse/muse/ruse
  d cute, include/intrude
  e rude/ruse/rule, exclude
  f prune, crude/chute
  g flute, crude/chute

COMMON WORDS >

1 **a** want; **b** under; **c** ran; **d** say; **e** tell
3 crude, flute, fuse, intrude, ran, rule, say, tell, under, want

Unit 15 REVISION

1 hate, mate, pine, kite, mope, pope, slide, rage, cute, grime, cope, made
2 pin, slid, slop, mop, rid, hat, cut, hop, us
3 **a** kite; **b** mat, bone; **c** pine; **d** slope; **e** cut; **f** made; **g** hide
4 Many answers; for example: stake, lime, pride, etc.
5 a Possible answers: ride, rode
  b Possible answers: home, cope
  c Possible answers: hive, stripe
  d Possible answers: stake, place
6 Possible answers: mine, line; wade, grade; flute, lute; mite, rite; rose, pose; face, trace
7 hate, bone, bike, nose, mice, joke, crime, nude
8 **a** pane; **b** fuse; **c** prize; **d** rid; **e** mad

Unit 16

1 **a** fry; **b** try; **c** why; **d** My; **e** why,
2 fly, butterfly, cry, spy, fry, July, smile, sty, sky
3 **a** sky; **b** July; **c** cry; **d** sty
4 Possible answers: cry, why, fly, fry
5 **a** cry, dry; **b** by, my; **c** myself, deny; **d** why, pigsty
6 July, cry, why, dry, fly, butterfly, try, shy
7 try, deny, pry, my, cry, sky, fly, fry, spy

WORD KNOWLEDGE >

1 **a** her; **b** she; **c** he; **d** we; **e** they
2 **a** he; **b** she; **c** they; **d** it

COMMON WORDS >

1 year; **2** best; **3** came; **4** find; **5** another

Unit 17

1 **a** fright; **b** knight; **c** tight; **d** fight; **e** light, bright; **f** sight
2 fright, night, tight, flight, knight, fight
3 a fright/flight, might
  b fight, light/might/night/right/sight/tight
  c fight/light/might/night/right/sight/tight, fight/light/might/night/right/sight/tight
  d knight, bright/flight/fright/plight/slight
4 **a** light; **b** sight; **c** right; **d** fight
5 Possible answers: might, fight, tight, right
6 right, fright, plight, fight, night, sight
7 highlight, knight, flight, twilight, slight, insight, alight, bright, delight, alright

WORD KNOWLEDGE >

1 **a** get; **b** put; **c** tidy; **d** brush; **e** eat; **f** wave

COMMON WORDS >

1 hand; **2** got; **3** leave; **4** near; **5** may

Unit 18

1 a knit, kneel, knuckle, knew, knee
  b wring, wrong, write
  c trip, bank
3 **a** knee; **b** knife; **c** wreck; **d** write; **e** wrinkle; **f** knock; **g** knots
4 **a** write/wrote; **b** wriggle; **c** knife; **d** knew/know; **e** wring/wrong; **f** wrinkle
5 Possible answers: know, wrote
6 kneel, knife, wrap, knuckle, wreck, knit
7 knees, wriggles, wrings, knows, knots, writes, knights, wrinkles, knocks
8 **a** knew; **b** write; **c** know; **d** wrong; **e** knit; **f** wring
9 **a** knife; **b** knob; **c** night; **d** knuckles; **e** wreck; **f** wrong

WORD KNOWLEDGE >

1 **a** licking; **b** sniffing; **c** miaowing; **d** flapping; **e** drinking; **f** shouting

COMMON WORDS >

1 **a** read; **b** school; **c** than; **d** open; **e** play
3 knife, knock, know, open, play, read, school, than, write, wrong

Unit 19

1 climb, calf, walk, limb, hand, salmon, fork, stalk, thumb
3 a numb; b walk; c calf; d psalm; e thumb; f limb; g lamb; h half
4 a crumb; b climb; c numb; d walk; e salmon; f talk
5 lamb, calm, talk, folk, half, numb
6 folk, crumb, dumb, palm, salmon, climb, talk, psalm
7 folks, walks, crumbs, limbs, climbs, stalks, bombs
8 a bomb; b folk; c comb; d calf; e talk; f lamb
9 a comb; b lamb; c climb; d walk; e calf; f numb; g half

WORD KNOWLEDGE >

1 a lived; b growled; c licked; d roared; e gobbled; f jumped; g shouted

COMMON WORDS >

1 a way; b until; c again; d be; e did
3 again, be, bomb, did, half, lamb, talk, until, walk, way

Unit 20 REVISION

1 b Possible answers: night, might, tight
c Possible answers: write, wrote, wriggle
d Possible answers: numb, limb, bomb
e Possible answers: kneel, knife, knot
f Possible answers: walk, folk, yolk
2 a climb; b knew; c night; d walk; e wriggle; f tight; g fry
3 calf, comb, plane, July, fly, knee, knit, lamb, thumb, knife, wriggle, fight
4 a sigh; b bone; c cow; d kit
5 Many answers; for example: brighten, knack, climb, wreck, etc.
6 a Possible answers: fry, cry
b Possible answers: try, pry
c Possible answers: by, my
d Possible answers: kneel, knuckle
e Possible answers: wrinkle, wriggle
f Possible answers: know, knew
g Possible answers: salmon, wrong
h Possible answers: kneel, knew
7 spy, sty, fly; night, sight, tight; knot, know, knob; fry, cry, dry

Unit 21

1 teeth; street, greet, sweet; greed, speed; queen, green, screen; weep, sleep, creep; bee, free, tree; week, peek; heel, wheel
3 a feed; b meet; c steel; d steep; e three; f week; g seen; h weed; i been
4 weep, heel, seed, green, cheek, fleet
5 a meat; b weak; c sea; d creak; e real; f sweat
6 a creek; b greed; c peek; d greet; e wheel; f screen
7 Possible answers: week, weep, green, feed, see, heel, greet, seek, sheep, sleet, keep, thee, greet, creek, meet, feet, seen, green

COMMON WORDS >

1 a high; b never; c right; d more; e please
3 high, jeep, more, never, please, right, speed, sweet, week, wheel

Unit 22

1 teeth; cream, scream, dream; mean, lean, clean; eagle; neat, beat, seat; speak, beak, weak; leaf; please
2 a beak; b scream; c dream; d seat; e beach; f steam; g leak; h teach; i beat
3 seat, mean, peach, neat, clean, weak
4 a leak; b peach; c lean; d please; e weak
5 a creep; b seem; c learn; d best; e beef; f week
6 a please; b weak; c scream; d feast; e dream; f eagle
7 Possible answers: least, teach, neat, mean, heat, beach, feast

COMMON WORDS

1 a name; b sad; c seem; d bit; e race
3 bit, clean, ice cream, name, please, race, reach, sad, seem, speak

Unit 23

1 a show; b grow/crow; c blow/glow/flow/slow; d blow/glow/flow/slow; e grow/crow; f yellow/pillow/bellow; g know; h below; i blow/glow/flow/slow; j elbow; k borrow/burrow
2 a low; b arrow; c slow; d window; e tomorrow
3 crow, snow, pillow, yellow, grow, tow
4 a show/slow; b rainbow; c show/slow; d pillow; e elbow; f row; g below; h tomorrow
5 a beach; b yesterday; c sheet; d go; e above; f groan
6 a grow; b arrow; c know; d window; e borrow; f row; g tow; h tomorrow
7 Possible answers: crow, yellow, flow, low, borrow

WORD KNOWLEDGE >

1 acorn, fecther, hamburger, eagle, juggle, bcot, dolphin, cut, iron, ghost
2 fish, girl, learn, letter, mango, market, necklace, net, oil, old, paddle, picture, rice, sad, sage, toea, touch, up, us, wall, worm

COMMON WORDS >

1 a found; b live; c book; d morning; e both
3 below, book, both, found, grow, know, live, morning, own, show

Unit 24

1 boat, soap, moan, toast, loaf, goat, coat, oats, road
2 a soap; b road; c load; d coach; e loaf; f moan; g boat; h throat; i toast
3 a boat; b float; c loaf; d boast; e road; f groan
4 goat, throat, coat, soap, float, moan
5 b floats, floating, floated
c loads, loading, loaded
d foams, foaming, foamed
e groans, groaning, groaned
f toasts, toasting, toasted
g boasts, boasting, boasted
h moans, moaning, moaned
7 a road; b coach; c soap; d throat; e foam; f oats
8 Possible answers: loan, moan, toad, toast, foam

WORD KNOWLEDGE >

boast, boat, coach, coat, float, foam, goat, groan, load, loaf, loan, moan, moat, oats, road, soap, throat, toast

COMMON WORDS >

1 a over; b present; c night
3 coach, coat, day, groan, night, over, present, road, shall, soap

Unit 25 REVISION

1 b Possible answers: seat, cheat, feat
c Possible answers: flow, show, mow
d Possible answers: boat, coat, throat
e Possible answers: need, feed, deed
f Possible answers: team, seam, scream

2 **a** row; **b** toast; **c** tree; **d** peel; **e** teach; **f** weak; **g** meat; **h** crow

3 **a** groan; **b** road; **c** meet; **d** creek; **e** sheet

4 Possible answers: yellow, toast, coach, teach, cream, meat, feast, pillow, toad, tow, seek, been, flow, moats

5 Many answers; for example: sheep, scream, throat, rowing, etc.

6 b seeds, seeding, seeded
c coats, coating, coated
d greets, greeting, greeted
e steams, steaming, steamed
f rows, rowing, rowed

7 low, row, tow; weep, jeep, deep; feed, need, seed

Unit 26

1 teeth; train, plain, main, chain, grain, stain; hail, pail, fail, mail; maid, paid, afraid, laid; paint, faint

3 **a** chain; **b** afraid; **c** train; **d** pail; **e** bait; **f** stain; **g** tail; **h** sail; **i** paint; **j** paid

4 paint, hail, mail, afraid, wait, brain

5 **a** paint **b** fail; **c** pain; **d** wail; **e** stain; **f** faint

6 **a** paint; **b** sale; **c** maid; **d** gale; **e** tram

7 **a** chain; **b** wait; **c** paint; **d** afraid; **e** stain; **f** tail

8 Possible answers: fail, maid, train, faint, wait, sail

WORD KNOWLEDGE >

1 into, breakfast, sunshine, football

2 **a** grandma; **b** pineapple; **c** peanut; **d** chalkboard; **e** cupboard; **f** grandpa; **g** necklace; **h** outrigger

COMMON WORDS >

1 **a** air; **b** change; **c** any; **d** great; **e** good

3 afraid, air, any, brain, change, good, great, paid, paint, sail

Unit 27

1 stay/slay, Sunday, relay, yesterday, slay, pray/play, runway, Friday, birthday, Wednesday, ray

2 **a** play; **b** ray; **c** Sunday; **d** runway; **e** Wednesday; **f** hay; **g** bay; **h** birthday; **i** relay

3 hay, pay, ray, today, pray, yesterday

4 **a** relay; **b** runway; **c** bay; **d** pay; **e** today; **f** yesterday; **g** pray

5 **a** train; **b** weekend; **c** steak; **d** slay; **e** great; **f** June

6 **a** stay; **b** runway; **c** slay; **d** relay

7 Possible answers: stay, relay, say, pray, play

WORD KNOWLEDGE >

1 sunspot, sunbake sunscreen, sundial, sunstroke, sunburn, suntan, sunglasses, sunlight, sunset, sunshade

2 Possible answers: playground, playschool, playmate, playbook, playtime

COMMON WORDS >

1 **a** water; **b** now; **c** first; **d** down; **e** my

3 birthday, down, first, may, my, now, play, stay, today, water

Unit 28

1 boil, coil, oil, spoil, foil; joint, point; coin, join; rejoice, voice, choice; moist

3 **a** oil; **b** coiled; **c** hoist; **d** spoil; **e** coin; **f** voice; **g** noise; **h** boil; **i** join

4 **a** boy; **b** spike; **c** trail; **d** staying; **e** nice

5 **a** broil; **b** point; **c** join; **d** choice; **e** oil; **f** boil

6 b foils, foiled, foiling
c boils, boiled, boiling
d joins, joined, joining
e points, pointed, pointing
f coils, coiled, coiling

7 spoil, coil, point, coin, moist, voice

8 **a** coin; **b** oil; **c** spoil; **d** join; **e** noise; **f** rejoice

WORD KNOWLEDGE >

1 they're, we've, it's, mustn't, you're, they've, didn't

2 **a** can't; **b** It's; **c** He's; **d** Don't; **e** didn't; **f** we're; **g** Let's

COMMON WORDS >

1 **a** bring; **b** could; **c** tree; **d** think; **e** white

3 boiled, bring, could, join, noise, spoil, think, tree, voice, white

Unit 29

1 joy, toys, enjoy, employ, annoy, oyster, boy, joyful, royal

2 **a** toy; **b** boy; **c** annoy; **d** voyage; **e** employ; **f** enjoy; **g** oyster; **h** toys

3 annoy, voyage, joy, destroy, boy, employ

4 **a** annoy; **b** enjoy; **c** boy; **d** royal; **e** toys; **f** loyal; **g** voyage; **h** joyful; **i** coy

5 **a** blow; **b** finger; **c** noisy; **d** girls; **e** coin; **f** voice

6 **a** royal; **b** loyal; **c** joy; **d** coy; **e** boy; **f** enjoyed; **g** employing

7 a loyal, boy/coy/joy/toy
b annoy, enjoy
c royal, toys
d coy, voyage

WORD KNOWLEDGE >

1 I'm, isn't, we're, didn't, let's

2 **b** it is; **c** we have; **d** you are; **e** I have

COMMON WORDS >

1 **a** five; **b** too; **c** mother; **d** house; **e** soon

3 boy, enjoy, five, house, loyal, mother, oyster, soon, too, toy

Unit 30 REVISION

1 b Possible answers: bay, hay, lay
c Possible answers: toil, soil, foil
d Possible answers: coy, destroy, toy
e Possible answers: Thursday, Friday, Saturday
f Possible answers: annoys, boys, employs

2 **a** enjoyed; **b** paint; **c** boil; **d** destroy; **e** voyage; **f** tail; **g** play; **h** stain

3 **a** draw; **b** July; **c** stray; **d** loyal; **e** great

4 Possible answers: train, moist, boys, maid, toil, faint, play, bait, playing

5 Many answers; for example: brain, stays, moist, enjoys, etc.

6 b enjoys, enjoyed, enjoying
c sails, sailed, sailing
d spoils, spoiled, spoiling
e boils, boiled, boiling
f stays, stayed, staying

7 boil, coil, coin; brain, train, grain; boy, toy, coy; paid, pail, fail

Unit 31

1 **a** how; **b** giant; **c** flow; **d** pray; **e** jump; **f** floor

2 draw, seesaw, raw, chainsaw, jaw, straw, claw, pawpaw

3 **a** caw; **b** paw; **c** pawpaw; **d** gnaw; **e** straw; **f** jigsaw; **g** seesaw; **h** outlaw
4 claw, draw, gnaw, law, paw, raw, saw, straw
5 **a** paw; **b** draw; **c** squaw; **d** straw; **e** chainsaw; **f** pawpaw
6 raw, saw, draw, straw, drawer
7 **b** raw; **c** straw; **d** seesaw

WORD KNOWLEDGE >

1 **a** loudly; **b** softly; **c** brightly; **d** suddenly; **e** quickly; **f** slowly

COMMON WORDS >

1 **a** why; **b** friend; **c** such; **d** ball; **e** stand
3 ball, claw, draw, friend, jaw, pawpaw, stand, such, thaw, why

Unit 32

1 **a** fish; **b** diamond; **c** stand; **d** know; **e** letter; **f** soup
2 stew, new, threw, grew, jewel, dew, chew, corkscrew
3 **a** blew; **b** threw; **c** jewel; **d** screw; **e** stew; **f** new; **g** drew
5 brew, chew, crew, drew, few, knew, pew, screw
6 **a** blew; **b** screw; **c** stew; **d** flew; **e** drew; **f** corkscrew; **g** grew; **h** dew
7 **a** knew; **b** grew; **c** blew; **d** threw; **e** drew
8 **a** new; **b** blew; **c** screw; **d** crew; **e** flew; **f** brew; **g** few

WORD KNOWLEDGE >

1 **a** gently; **b** loudly; **c** quickly; **d** quietly; **e** greedily

COMMON WORDS >

1 **a** sure; **b** brown; **c** carry; **d** along; **e** wish
3 along, brown, carry, flew, grew, jewel, knew, new, sure, wish

Unit 33

1 **a** brush; **b** anywhere; **c** roar; **d** shadow; **e** sandals; **f** lions
2 clown, crowd, cow, flower, towel, shower
3 **a** shower; **b** towel; **c** growl; **d** how; **e** flower; **f** owl
5 crow, crown, drown, town, flower, flown, gown, grower, growl, grown, how, howl, prow, prowl, shower, shown, tower
6 **a** crowd; **b** owl; **c** tower; **d** growl; **e** clown; **f** towel
8 **a** cow; **b** how; **c** clown; **d** owl; **e** now; **f** frown; **g** flower; **h** crown

WORD KNOWLEDGE >

1 **a** along; **b** through; **c** beside; **d** onto; **e** into; **f** over

COMMON WORDS >

1 **a** hid; **b** down; **c** easy; **d** gave; **e** face
3 crowd, didn't, down, easy, face, flower, gave, hid, power, somehow

Unit 34

1 **a** crowd; **b** kitchen; **c** coconut; **d** fork; **e** jungle; **f** seem
2 pool, moon, hoot, noon, cool, food
3 **a** moon; **b** goose; **c** kangaroo; **d** balloon; **e** spoon; **f** roof
5 boom, boot, brood, broom, food, fool, foot, good, goof, goon, goose, hood, hoof, hoon, hoot, noon, noose, roof, room, root, soon, soot, zoom
6 **a** root; **b** roof; **c** pool; **d** moon; **e** shoot
8 **a** moon; **b** noon; **c** soon; **d** balloon; **e** broom

WORD KNOWLEDGE >

1 **a** because; **b** so; **c** and; **d** before; **e** but

COMMON WORDS >

1 **a** letter; **b** run; **c** might; **d** keep; **e** jump
3 cool, food, jump, keep, letter, might, roof, run, spoon, tooth

Unit 35 REVISION

1 Possible answers: **b** drew; **c** frown; **d** soot; **e** flower; **f** seesaw; **g** noon
2 **a** flower; **b** mood; **c** knew; **d** raw; **e** crowd; **f** screw
3 **a** growl; **b** chew; **c** eyebrow; **d** straw; **e** clown
4 cow, seesaw, tooth, jigsaw, clown, eyebrow, claw, crown, moon, jewel, bedroom, goose, shoot, boot, growl, balloon
5 Many answers; for example: jewel, knew, strawberry, flaw, crown, spoon, etc.
6 **a** claw; **b** goose; **c** growl; **d** cow; **e** broom; **f** crown; **g** towel; **h** new
7 howl, prowl, growl; grew, chew; roof; tooth; claw, paw; crown, down, brown; boot; loose; food; jewel; moon, balloon; zoom; power
8 **b** claws, clawed, clawing
c prowls, prowled, prowling
d stews, stewed, stewing

Unit 36

1 **a** pool; **b** boil; **c** cloud; **d** straw; **e** flower; **f** blew
2 chair, hairy, airport, pair, repair, fair, fairy, air
3 **a** airstrip; **b** chair; **c** air; **d** fairytale; **e** hair; **f** airbag; **g** pair
4 **a** chair; **b** stairs; **c** wheelchair; **d** hair; **e** airmail; **f** hairy
5 Possible answers: hair, stair, fairy, repair, hairy, stairs, chair, dairy
6 **a** chair; **b** stairs; **c** hairy; **d** fairy; **e** dairy; **f** air
8 **a** chair; **b** fairy; **c** hairy; **d** air; **e** hair; **f** dairy

WORD KNOWLEDGE >

1 **a** day; **b** out; **c** girl; **d** down; **e** no; **f** cold
2 **a** slow; **b** deep; **c** dry; **d** cold; **e** right

COMMON WORDS >

1 **a** o'clock; **b** seven; **c** ride; **d** same; **e** second
3 air, chair, hair, o'clock, pair, ride, same, second, seven, stairs

Unit 37

1 **a** chair; **b** airport; **c** pork; **d** airbag; **e** sunlight; **f** firm
2 star, shark, carpet, jar, dark, car, March
3 **a** start; **b** shark; **c** car; **d** farm; **e** starlight; **f** party
4 **a** park; **b** arm; **c** start; **d** park; **e** party; **f** shark
5 bark, barn, cart, farm, park, part, party, smart, stark, start
6 **a** carport; **b** dark; **c** barn; **d** mark; **e** jar; **f** start; **g** park
7 **a** park; **b** bar; **c** barn; **d** mark; **e** part; **f** art; **g** start; **h** tart; **i** marks; **j** bark; **k** arm; **l** star

WORD KNOWLEDGE >

1 **a** excellent, great, clever, lovely
b little, tiny
c rotten, naughty
d shouted, screamed
2 ocean, sea; cup, mug; cry, sob; cool, cold; run, sprint

COMMON WORDS >

1 **a** always; **b** yellow; **c** think; **d** walk; **e** buy
3 always, buy, dark, harm, mark, party, smart, think, walk, yellow

Unit 38

1 **a** dark; **b** barn; **c** sharp; **d** ice cream; **e** south; **f** smell
2 short, horn, storm, north, torn
3 **a** horse; **b** thunderstorm; **c** corn; **d** short; **e** corner; **f** torch; **g** north; **h** popcorn; **i** sport
4 **a** born; **b** for; **c** horse; **d** force; **e** worn; **f** corner
5 Many answers; for example: short, torch, worm, north, etc.
6 **a** morning; **b** storm; **c** short; **d** torch; **e** sport; **f** short; **g** worn
7 **a** for; **b** north; **c** corn; **d** force; **e** horse; **f** torn; **g** fort; **h** horn; **i** sort

WORD KNOWLEDGE ›

1 **a** uneven; **b** unhappy; **c** unpack; **d** unwise; **e** unsafe; **f** unable
3 **a** dislike; **b** disappear; **c** disagree; **d** disinfect; **e** disobey; **f** displace

COMMON WORDS ›

1 **a** eight; **b** clean; **c** goes; **d** door; **e** fall
3 born, clean, corner, door, eight, fall, force, goes, north, storm

Unit 39

1 **a** show; **b** crowd; **c** crawl; **d** enjoy; **e** boil; **f** today
2 hood, cook, book, wool, hook, wood, cookbook
6 **a** good; **b** soot; **c** hook; **d** shook; **e** cook; **f** book; **g** took
3 **a** wood/wool; **b** cookbook; **c** hook; **d** firewood
5 Many answers; for example: shoot, crook, good, wool, etc.
6 **a** good; **b** soot; **c** hook; **d** shook; **e** cook; **f** book; **g** took

WORD KNOWLEDGE ›

1 **a** looked; **b** climbed; **c** played; **d** pushed; **e** kicked; **f** worked
2 **a** eating; **b** blowing; **c** crying; **d** kneeling; **e** shouting; **f** licking

COMMON WORDS ›

1 **a** hear; **b** longer; **c** third; **d** off; **e** show
3 book, good, hear, longer, off, shook, show, stood, third, wool

Unit 40 REVISION

1 Possible answers: **b** farming; **c** corn; **d** took; **e** normal; **f** chair; **g** look
2 **a** carport; **b** sport; **c** wool; **d** airstrip; **e** hairy; **f** shark; **g** good; **h** hair
3 **a** crowd; **b** farmyard; **c** moonlight; **d** south; **e** wind
4 chair, book, hair, fairy, shoot, cook, horse, jar, short, shark
5 Many answers; for example: dairy, park, forget, took, etc.
6 **a** born; **b** cook; **c** short; **d** fairy; **e** torch; **f** dark; **g** corn; **h** start
7 hook, cook, shook, book, wood, wool; art, harm, arm, party, starlight, carport; torch, force, horse, morning, carport, sport, popcorn; hair, chair, repair, dairy, fair
8 **b** cooks, cooked, cooking
c parks, parked, parking
d marks, marked, marking
e pairs, paired, pairing
f airs, aired, airing
g corners, cornered, cornering
h sorts, sorted, sorting